FS Books:
Sportsman's Best: Inshore Fishing
Sportsman's Best: Offshore Fishing
Sportsman's Best: Snapper & Grouper
Sportsman's Best: Sailfish
Sportsman's Best: Trout
Sportsman's Best: Redfish
Sportsman's Best: Dolphin

Sport Fish of Florida
Sport Fish of the Gulf of Mexico
Sport Fish of the Atlantic
Sport Fish of Fresh Water
Sport Fish of the Pacific

Baits, Rigs & Tackle
Annual Fishing Planner
The Angler's Cookbook

Florida Sportsman Magazine
Shallow Water Angler Magazine
Florida Sportsman Fishing Charts
Lawsticks
Law Boatstickers

Author, Rick Ryals
Edited by Florida Sportsman Staff
Art Director, Drew Wickstrom
Illustrations by Joe Suroviec
Copy Edited by Sam Hudson
Photos by Scott Sommerlatte, Joe Richard, Pat Ford, SaltyShores.com,
Jason Arnold, Tony Ludovico

DOLPHIN

CONTENTS

SB

SPORTSMAN'S BEST
DOLPHIN

10

Savannah

32

Atlantic
Ocean

Tampa

Miami

Bahamas

58

70

Stand back—mayhem's about to break loose. It's a big part of the excitement of catching these powerful fish.

Foreword

Lessons from Dolphin School

They've always been dolphin to me. Porpoise was Flipper, the mammal. No confusion. No need for name changes to mahi mahi or dorado. My first run-in with a dolphin school, nearly four decades ago, on our family's 20-foot cuddy cabin still seems like last weekend. You couldn't have asked for a better introduction to offshore fishing—three 8- to 10-year-olds all hooked up, fish jumping, dad screaming, fish flopping and blood flying. Awesome. Dolphin.

Because of the dolphin's need to feed and unbelievable growth rate, the species will continue to make similar impressions on offshore anglers around the world. This perpetual hunger sometimes makes dolphin seem pretty indiscriminate about what and how they'll eat, often being tagged with the "dumb fish" label. The fact is they're not dumb, just young—and hungry. A school-size dolphin can be as young as 8 to 10 weeks.

In order to catch the old and cagy fish, the 3-year-olds, it takes a little more than ballyhoo chunks and strips of squid. These fish are just as hungry, but not as easily found or caught. They can also be up to six feet long and more than 70 pounds.

Sportsman's Best: Dolphin will go into detail on how you can better your odds of catching the biggest of the 'phins, the super slammers. Fortunately it doesn't require going to exotic locales in the southern hemisphere; these big fish swim the same waters as the peanuts, often feeding on them. The one thing that does change when targeting these big fish is the tackle you're using.

Many anglers, myself included, feel that dolphin are one of the strongest, hardest-fighting fish in the ocean. They can dog you like an AJ, jump higher and more often than a sailfish and swim with the explosive bursts of a tuna. The truth is most people equate dolphin fights with the smaller fish most often caught.

For the biggest dolphin, there's no room to underestimate their power. You'll need tackle set up for large offshore fish. You'll need a crew that's ready for the task at hand: someone who can keep the boat in the correct position, someone ready to make the gaff shot and someone ready to direct the fish into the box. Or, if you're like most of us, fishing with family and friends with varying degrees of angling experience, you'll need a crew willing to roll up their sleeves and have some fun. Be ready for some OTJ (On The Job) training, screaming, laughing, missing, re-positioning, second and third tries, and finally, hopefully, bringing a catch of a lifetime over the gunnel.

There's no better fish in the sea for making a lifetime of memories, but don't be fooled: To catch the big ones consistently you'll have to be more than lucky, and that's what author Capt. Rick Ryals and the editors of *Florida Sportsman* have set out to do for you with this book and DVD, to give you the information you need to bring home dolphin.

— Blair Wickstrom, Publisher, *Florida Sportsman* Magazine

Rich gold stored in our memory banks, those vivid colors never fade.

Hooked on the First Strike

I t had been three hours since the last of my fishing buddies deserted the stern of the 65-foot motor sailor for the comfort of the salon. The sun had risen to 30 degrees on the horizon, and the slick ocean reflected pure summer heat on my 15-year-old face. The year was 1968, and I was on the first bluewater overnight trip of my life.

When we left Mayport, Florida at midnight the night before, our six-man crew could hardly wait to reach blue water. I guess none of us was smart enough to realize, at a maximum cruise speed of eight knots, we should have slept while we sloshed the 60 miles to the edge of the Gulf Stream like a high-speed toadfish. When nobody had even seen a fish by 9:30 the next morning, I was left alone to tend the lines. Within minutes of being abandoned, I started to see the first flyingfish skitter across the shiny surface like a flushed quail. To this day, nothing excites me like the sights and sounds of bluewater trolling.

Sensing something was about to happen, I began to mentally perform the "dropback" technique, which I had practiced like an air guitar, but never tried on the water. Back then, my exposure to deep-sea fishing had been for kingfish with spoons. Trolling natural baits was something pros did.

Suddenly, the telltale wake I've loved ever since came cutting in from under a patch of grass. He was after my bonito strip which was surely washed out from hours of fruitless dragging. Without a single witness to what I later narrated as a perfect dropback, the 10-pound dolphin took to the air. My love affair with the green and gold was on, full-bore.

It was many years, and many dolphin later, that I began to understand what amazing fish these are. I certainly didn't know my 10-pound fish was only a few months old. I didn't understand what it had been doing under that patch of grass, or that it may have just ridden a southeast breeze in from the middle of the ocean.

The "greatest gamefish" has been debated since the first trolled bait hit the water. Who among us wouldn't put dolphin on the list, anywhere they're available?

Let's review. They're gorgeous. They're fast. They jump like crazy. They're delicious. They can be incredibly abundant and easy to catch one day, yet totally frustrating the next.

We all know the old truism is true about 10 percent of the people catching 90 percent of the fish. It's just as true with dolphin as anything else. To be successful you'll need to know where and when to look for them, and you'll need to know how to get them to bite when they've already seen the baits from a hundred boats.

Fair warning, though. I've been lying awake the night before every bluewater trip for the last 30 years. Among all the fish that can keep me up all night, dolphin are right at the top.

—Rick Ryals

CHAPTER 1

The Perfect Pelagic

Arguably no other pelagic species inspires as many anglers to venture offshore as the mighty dolphin. Few sights in angling can rival a lit-up bull dolphin charging through a spread. They fight acrobatically—all the way to the cooler. They can even break off a cooler lid at the hinges, if "green" enough. And when kept ice-cold, the culinary reward for the fishing expedition is exquisite.

Dolphin are prolific, but not invincible. Fortunately, recognizing the species' value to the recreational fishing community, the U.S. National Marine Fisheries Service (NMFS) created a management plan with a goal to stabilize harvest levels and ensure that no new commercial fisheries develop. Our domestic dolphin fisheries have historically been recreational fisheries, and with current protections in place, so should they remain.

Dolphin can fill fish boxes from Rio de Janeiro to Nova Scotia. Responsible anglers are learning to keep only enough to last them until the next trip.

See DVD for more on the perfect pelagic.

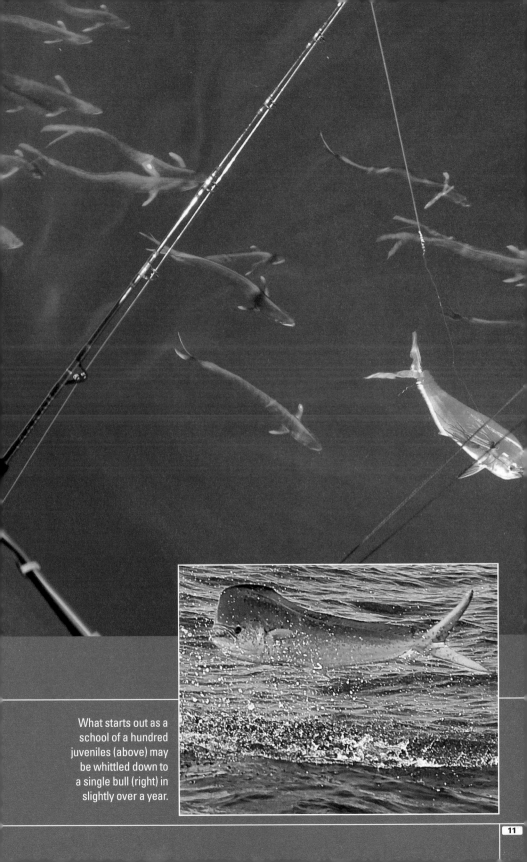

What starts out as a school of a hundred juveniles (above) may be whittled down to a single bull (right) in slightly over a year.

Anywhere, Any Tackle

Dolphin are the perfect pelagic gamefish. Plentiful and wide-ranging, they have fans all over the world who call them by many names. Dolphin show up in fish boxes from Georges Bank south to Rio de Janeiro. Actually, they are a circumtropical species, occurring throughout the world's tropical and warm-temperate ocean waters: in the Atlantic, Pacific and Indian oceans; as well as in the Caribbean, Adriatic and Mediterranean seas; and the Sea of Japan. Depending on depths, you may find dolphin anywhere from a mile offshore out to the middle of the ocean.

Actually, there are two species of dolphin, the common dolphin (*Coryphaena hippurus*) and the diminutive pompano dolphin (*C. equiselis*). Many of the schools of smaller dolphin anglers encounter are actually pompano dolphin. These little eating machines, or "green hornets" as offshore trollers call them, are the common dolphin's little cousin. Rarely exceeding 5 pounds, the pompano dolphin are usually encountered many miles offshore.

At first glance the two species are easily confused, but the pompano dolphin has a higher profile than a small common dolphin. The tallest part of the pompano dolphin body is in the middle, while a young common dolphin is tallest just behind the head. The pectoral fins of a pompano dolphin are smaller, and the dorsal fin is fuller and shorter. The common dolphin can also be distinguished from the pompano dolphin by its body depth. Body depth of the common dolphin is less than 25 percent of its length, while the pompano dolphin body depth is greater than 25 percent.

Regardless of size or species, dolphin are acrobatic fighters and mesmerizing to see. Their kaleidoscopic range of colors dazzles the eye, no matter how many times you've seen one live, on the hook or free-swimming by your boat along a weedline. You can catch them on almost any kind of tackle, including conventional trolling tackle, spinning tackle, plug tackle and fly rods. And you can find them small enough for the grandkids to reel in, and big enough to strip line against the tightest drag on a 50-wide.

Get to Know Your Catch

The males or "bull" dolphin have square heads, while the cows (females) have rounded heads. Glands called "chromataphors" give dolphin the ability to change colors, and flash neon spots and fluorescent bars given change in mood. They really light up when they move into your spread, excited by foraging opportunities. But they are especially prized because of their relative abundance and delicious flesh. We all look forward to taking a few home.

As rarely as dolphin of this size visit your bait spread, it's sometimes hard to remember an adult fish may be less than a year old.

You Name It

Anglers have many nicknames for dolphin including "slammer" for a big dolphin; "gaffer" for fish large enough to warrant the hook; and "peanut," "bailer," or "chicken" for small fish.

If you ask your wife to fry the kids up a couple of bailers, roll a couple of bacon strips in some flour, sauté some slingers, and stuff a piece of slammer with some crab meat, you must be a dolphin fisherman.

Bacon strips, named for the size of fillet you can take off each side (remember size and bag limits) make up the bottom of the dolphin size range. Slightly bigger than the bacon strip, the bailer requires no special tools, like gaffs, to welcome them aboard. It's easy to just grab the leader and sling them in the box (hence the name slingers).

Slightly bigger than a bailer, a schoolie dolphin usually doesn't require a gaff, but is generally not in packs of more than 20 fish. These fish are normally in the 5- to 8-pound range.

From Carolina through the Caribbean, everybody welcomes the gaffers aboard. These fish are too big to sling over the rails. They are from 8 to 20 pounds, and they make up the bulk of most anglers' best fishing days.

The slammer's very name calls for the need to stick him in the box with one motion, and slam the lid shut with the other. Their thrashing tails have snapped many an ankle, and just because they don't have the teeth of a mackerel or barracuda, you don't want to get close.

Sling the slingers and bail the bailers, but slam the lid when the big boy hits the box. SB

Peanut s a.k.a. Bacon Strips, Grasshopper
Since most of these fish should be released, they are seldom targeted. But they eat just about anything, including ballyhoo chunks, pieces of squid, chicken tenders and baloney, as well as trolled baits nearly bigger than they are. Sometimes you just can't avoid them.

Mahi Mahi means strong, strong, and for good reason. Don't try to pose with a slammer until you know he's done thrashing.

Schoolie a.k.a. Bailer, Chicken

Definitely a legal fish, over 20 inches. Fun to catch on 12- to 15-pound tackle. Like their younger brother, Peanut, they travel in large schools and eat just about anything. The key to catching more than one is leaving a hooked fish in the water, keeping the school within casting range.

Gaffer 10 to 20 Pounds

Early spring is your best chance at finding a school of Gaffer dolphin, which will make any skipper's day. And as the name implies your best chance of boating one of these fish is with a well-placed gaff shot. Will readily respond to chunks, at or near the boat, but most are caught trolling.

SLAMMERS/ SUPER SLAMMERS

At 20 to 40 pounds, dolphin begin to pair up and leave the schools. Large trolled baits, or a fortunate find where you can toss a live bait, are your best chances at a Slammer. And as you might expect, you'll need to be ready to "slam" the door of your fish box closed once you bring your fish on board.

The so-called Super Slammers, 40 to 80 pounds, still aren't even four years old, but will fight as hard as any fish in the ocean. You better have your tackle in good condition. If possible, forgo the spinners and grab a 50-wide. Trolling large baits is key to catching this fish of a lifetime. SB

CHAPTER 2

The Dolphinfish

Scientists' descriptions of an animal's physiology, life history and growth rates are often cautious and understated. Not so when they speak of the dolphinfish. They use words such as "dramatic," "remarkable" and even "exponential" to describe this fascinating fish, especially in the context of its growth rate and rapid sexual maturity.

Due to their tremendous oxygen needs, dolphin must swim continuously to ventilate their gills. In order to achieve such high gas exchange, dolphin gills have a larger surface area than those of most other bony fishes. As a result these fish expend more energy than most species. Therefore, dolphin must feed almost continuously.

Considering that the ocean is mostly an underwater desert, you'd think that surely no pelagic fish, especially a dolphin, could afford to pass up whatever you drag past it. Not so. By understanding the life history and feeding habits of dolphin, you can learn to make better presentations in the most productive areas.

Brian Sylvester Texas Mahi

The dolphin was made to be in art. No fish represents the rainbow any better. It can go from blue to green to purple and back to green in seconds.

Graham Hill
Steel dolphin
www.rockwood.com

Life History

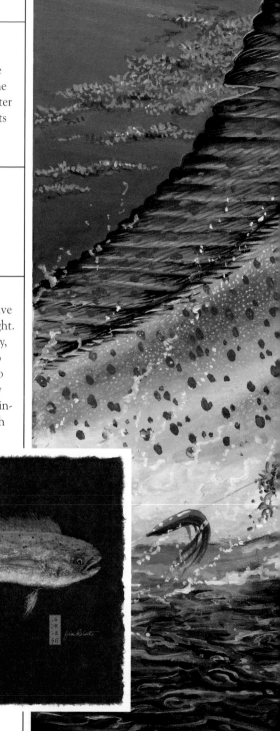

Dolphin spend the majority of their lives in water warmer than 70 degrees. While some biologists tend to discount the time dolphin spend near the bottom, several deepwater longliners have reported huge bulls on their baits set deeper than 200 feet. "Benthic" or bottom-dwelling organisms such as mantis shrimp are

Because they are pelagic and highly migratory, it is assumed that dolphin spawn on the fly, so to speak.

commonly found in their gut contents. Tagging studies by the Dolphinfish Research Program have documented that most deep diving occurs at night.

Because they are pelagic and highly migratory, it is assumed that dolphin spawn on the fly, so to speak. In other words, they don't show fidelity to specific spawning sites. But studies performed by the Dolphinfish Research Program (www.dolphin-tagging.com) show that dolphin spawn off South Carolina, as evidenced by the collection

Jim Roberts Cows on paper

Carey Chen
Big bull rodeo

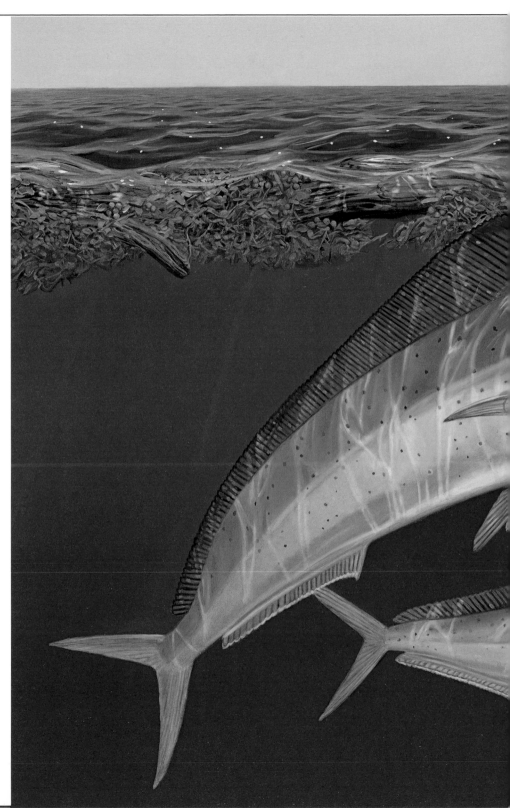

Randy McGovern
Dolphin on the fliers

Flying Fisherman
Hot on the Trail

Studies have shown that dolphin are capable of growing to a length of 4 feet and a weight of 40 pounds in less than a single year.

of early juvenile fish and adult fish in spawning condition from spring through fall. Temperature, and perhaps moon phases, may be more important than any spatial reference point. Dol-

phin are "batch spawners" as fertilization occurs externally as males and females discharge gametes together in the open ocean. A Florida study calculated that a female 39 inches in fork length produces roughly 555,000 eggs per spawn. It is thought they spawn at least three times per year.

Spawning seems to occur in the first 35 feet of deep blue water, and is believed to occur from spring through fall. Seventy-eight-to 82.4- degree water temperatures seem to get them in the mood. But it's quite possible that dolphin spawn year-round in warmer climes. According to the

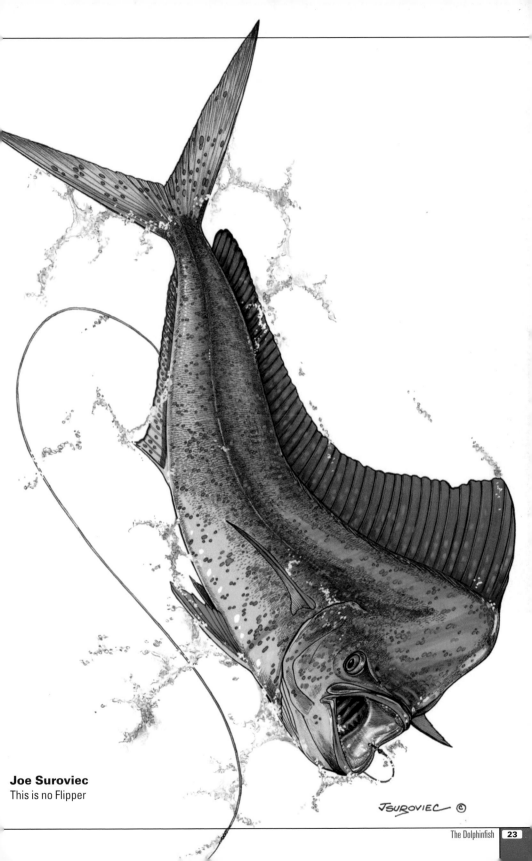

Joe Suroviec
This is no Flipper

JSUROVIEC ©

MARK JOHNSON

Mark Johnson
Deep blue zoo

Still, 98 to 99.7 percent of dolphin perish during their first year. Not only are they important forage species for every major predator, they have no qualms about eating each other.

Florida Museum of Natural History, researchers have documented dolphinfish larvae in the Florida Current year-round.

Larvae are pelagic and quickly develop into post-larval fishes. Post-larval dolphin instinctively associate with sargassum and other objects floating in the ocean, for food and protection from predators. Still, 98 to 99.7 percent of dolphin perish during their first year. Not only are they important forage species for every major predator, they have no qualms about eating each other.

If a larger percentage survived the juvenile life stages, we would probably be overrun by massive herds of yellow and green gangsters, until there was nothing left in the ocean for them to eat. The reality is that 2-year-old fish make up less

than 2 percent of the total population.

Dolphin are considered "apex" predators, but are by no means at the top of the food chain. Sooner or later, you will have a small- to mid-size dolphin attacked by a shark, large wahoo or a marlin. The smaller they are the more vulnerable they are to predation.

Studies have shown that dolphin are capable of growing to a length of 4 feet and a weight of 40 pounds in less than a single year. (Can you imagine growing at 1.3 to 2.7 inches per week?) Males, or bulls, grow at a faster rate than females, often weighing 20 percent more, and attaining up to 20 percent more length at the same age. Dolphin are sexually mature within two months of age. A 1-pound bull dolphin was placed in the tank at the

Guy Harvey Three's company

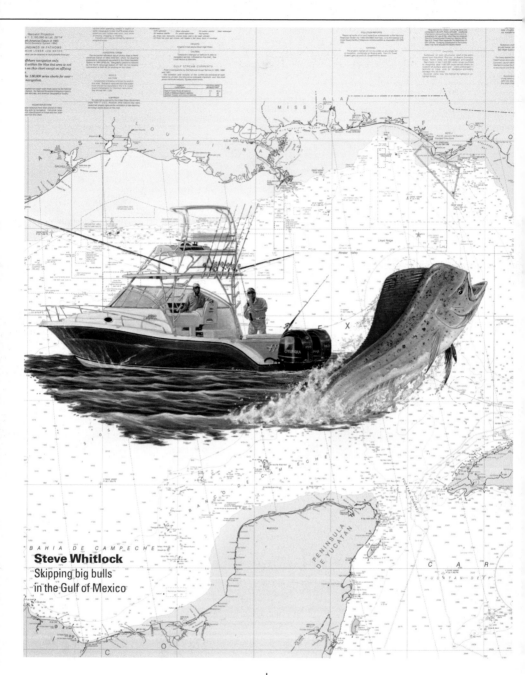

Steve Whitlock
Skipping big bulls
in the Gulf of Mexico

Miami Seaquarium and the fish grew to 32 pounds in 8 months. Females rarely exceed 40 pounds, while males routinely grow to 60 pounds. The record is 88 pounds, but in 1979 *Florida Sportsman* magazine reported a 101-pound fish caught off Puerto Rico.

The species is highly migratory and is known to travel as far as 800 miles in 10 days. However, certain features give them pause. As juveniles and adults, dolphin are drawn by any type of flotsam and jetsam, but are especially fond of sargassum. In many cases the biggest fish are caught along color changes and rips. Given their relative abundance, range and exponential growth rates, you stand a chance of breaking the world record every time you venture offshore. SB

Pasta Pantaleo
'06

Pasta Pantaleo
The Party's over

CHAPTER 3

A Fishery On the Move

To catch dolphin consistently, it helps to be in the right place at the right time, so it's time to learn a bit about oceanography. These travelers' lives are governed by the world's ocean currents, which are the strongest influence on sea-surface temperatures. The seasonal expansion and contraction of warm water dictates the extent of their range and when they will appear, or "run" off a given stretch of coast.

Cold water effectively limits the dolphin's latitudinal range, and quite possibly the species' vertical range in the water column. But the friction between coldwater upwelling and warm eddies cycles nutrients upward in the water column, which attracts zooplankton and in turn many of the dolphin's favorite food sources.

Remember, a fish doesn't know where it is, and doesn't care where it is. You'll need to learn the conditions that bring dolphin food and make them comfortable.

What could make a
better picture than
four pretty girls and
the most colorful fish
in the ocean?

Big bulls are normally surface feeders, but archival tags have shown they visit depths to 400 feet, particularly at night. Studies of stomach contents have shown squid as the most likely targets of deep divers.

Thermo Thinking

Yesterday's anglers had no temperature maps. When the old-timers came home with empty fish boxes, it meant they "weren't biting."

A difference in water color, or a color change, often marks a change in temperature. Experienced anglers know to work these food-rich edges. Ocean currents, tides and winds also create rips, which draw sargassum and other floating structure into a line. Bottom contours sometimes determine where a weedline forms, so a good sonar system can be an aid wherever in the world you target dolphin.

We have much to learn about the nearly worldwide distribution of both common and pompano dolphin. Unfortunately, tagging initiatives are fairly new, and data has been complex and difficult to decipher. One confounding factor in learning about dolphin migrations is that so few fish have been tagged and recaught.

What do we know? Dolphin inhabit all the world's major oceans, and it appears each ocean has a separate population of fish above and below the equator. However, there may be overlaps in populations between Atlantic and Caribbean fish, and in other places where a warm sea is contiguous to an ocean.

In the Atlantic, dolphin have been reported as far north as Ireland and as far south as the tip of Africa. Scientists generally agree dolphin in the northern hemisphere migrate north from the equator during the spring and summer then return south in the fall. Below the equator, the migration is southward in the antipodal summer months.

The world over, warm waters expand and contract to the north or south of the equator with the approach of each hemisphere's respective summer or winter months. As the warm-water regions expand or shrink, dolphin center their activity around 78.8- to 82.4-degree temperature envelope. In each hemisphere, dolphin range farthest to the north or south in the summers, when warm water covers a larger area of the respective oceanic latitudes. As fall and winter

approach, the hordes of "green hornets" follow warm water and bait migrations back toward the equator. The spring migration, away from the equator, is largely made up of schools of juveniles, usually accompanied by a few larger bulls and cows. After feeding throughout the spring, and growing like weeds, it's mostly packs of bigger adults that return to the equator come fall.

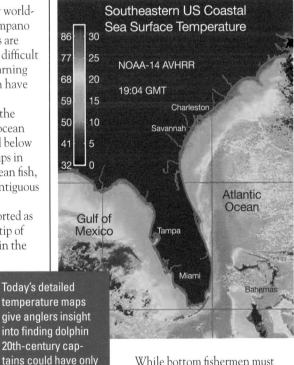

Southeastern US Coastal Sea Surface Temperature

NOAA-14 AVHRR

19:04 GMT

Charleston

Savannah

Atlantic Ocean

Gulf of Mexico

Tampa

Miami

Bahamas

Today's detailed temperature maps give anglers insight into finding dolphin 20th-century captains could have only dreamed of.

While bottom fishermen must focus mostly on structure, dolphin fishermen need also be "thermo-thinkers," because migrations are clearly triggered by water temperatures and the availability of forage. These eating machines can't stray far from the snack bar; starvation seems to be a major part of dolphin mortality.

Dolphin are only year-round residents in areas where water temperature stays above the

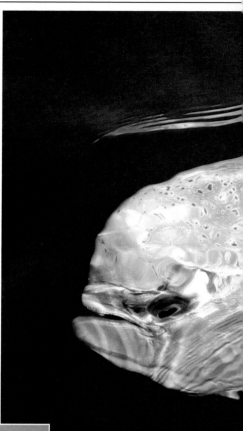

> **A dolphin spends almost its whole life in water between 78 and 82 degrees, a sudden drop of 2 degrees must be a huge shock.**

78.8-degree mark, and where the first hundred feet in the water column is clear and blue. Pronounced seasonal temperature variations occur in areas where water temp drops below 78.8 degrees during certain times of the year. NOAA's "Synopsis of the Biological Data on Dolphin" states that dolphin do not occur in areas with water temps less than 69.8 degrees. Therefore, it's important to know depths and the locations of bottom contours, which create rips and contribute to the formation of weedlines. But it is equally important to understand "isotherms," the lines connecting locations with equal temperature. Isotherm maps show where temperatures are relatively high and low, and also where temperature changes are gradual or dramatic over a distance.

Areas of the ocean with the same water temperatures are symbolized on temperature charts by a series of lines drawn on the ocean surface.

Unheard of in the United States, there are places where dolphin can be hooked within yards of shore.

Day-to-day movements as well as dolphin migrations can be accurately predicted by observing the movements of these isotherms and fishing within the species' temperature preferences. (For more on isotherms and temperature charts, see Chapter 11.)

The ability to turn broadside with a high profile means a dolphin will always provide a tougher battle on a rod and reel than any long, sleek fish of the same size.

The Proof Is in the Tag

Between 2002 and 2006, 4,900 North Atlantic dolphin were tagged and 116 were returned. In 2006, 1,500 dolphin were tagged by 260 recreational anglers on 143 boats. Forty-nine tags were returned. Results from these studies confirmed the south-to-north migration along the eastern U.S. seaboard. It also showed that fish from the southeastern Bahamas will even make their way up to the Hudson Canyon.

In 2006, funding for dolphin research had run out. Responsible anglers jumped in to fund more studies. Marine fisheries biologist Don Hammond started the Cooperative Science Services, LLC to continue research. Within a year, South Carolina Sea Grant Consortium and the South Carolina DNR began employing a hi-tech monitoring instrument known as a pop-off archival tag. Thanks to these tags, we know that dolphin dive as deep as 350 feet, often at night, presumably to feed on squid and other deepwater forage. We also have the beginnings of an understanding about their typical migration patterns. SB

When government funding for dolphin research ran out in 2006, responsible anglers stepped up funding to keep learning more about their life cycle and migrations.

International Dispersals of East Coast Fish

In 2006, 1,500 dolphin were tagged by 260 recreational anglers on 143 boats. Forty-nine tags were returned showing some unbelievable migrations. Green pennants here indicate area of tag and release; red circles represent sample of recaptures.

Florida

Release Sites

Atlantic Ocean

The Bahamas

Gulf of Mexico

April 06
252 days

Cuba

February 05
241 days

March 06
246 days

Yucatán Peninsula

April 05
330 days

Caribbean Sea

February 08
263 days

Venezuela

www.dolphintagging.com

Miles of weed, but which piece is hiding the fish?

Goals for Research Efforts in the Future

■ Increasing the number of vessels involved in tagging dolphin in the Mid-Atlantic Bight, the Gulf of Mexico, The Bahamas and throughout the Caribbean Sea.

■ Continue to study the relationship between dolphin and sargassum weed using tagged fish studies.

■ Determine what percentage of fish are harvested by anglers from each state, and by other user groups, such as commercial fishers.

■ Solicit more boats to tag dolphin off Florida in the summer and fall to determine the length and if there is a north-to-south migration in Florida.

■ Solicit more government as well as private funding for more pop-off satellite archival tags. Fishing clubs and organizations are being solicited to fund these tags to learn more about individual migrations as well as diving behavior.

■ Keep the public informed through the study's Web site, as well as regularly issued e-newsletters. Get pertinent information to fisheries management in charge of the Atlantic, Gulf of Mexico and Caribbean dolphin stocks.

■ Since the turn of the century we've made great strides in fisheries management, but the lion's share of the work remains in front of us. It's incumbent on us to err on the conservative side. You can do that by self-imposing a boat limit below the published limits.

■ And let's all support research and law enforcement efforts so our grandchildren—and their grandchildren—may witness more red-hot bull dolphin charging into the spread on a calm day. SB

Tagging returns have shown that if this young man had missed his strike, his big bull may well have been a hundred miles away by the next day.

Northerly Movements by Two Florida Fish

If a dolphin migrated 835 miles in 9 days, imagine how much water it actually covered.

1,197 Miles in 51 Days

North Carolina

835 Miles in 9 Days

South Carolina

Georgia

Atlantic Ocean

Florida

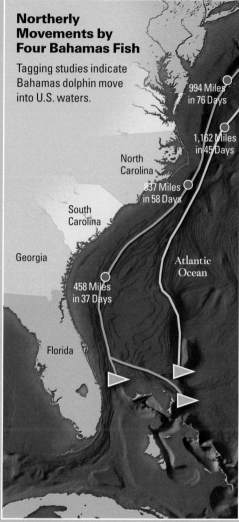

Northerly Movements by Four Bahamas Fish

Tagging studies indicate Bahamas dolphin move into U.S. waters.

994 Miles in 76 Days

1,162 Miles in 45 Days

North Carolina

837 Miles in 58 Days

South Carolina

Georgia

458 Miles in 37 Days

Atlantic Ocean

Florida

www.dolphintagging.com

Dolphin on the Move

Prior to 1990, North Atlantic dolphin were primarily targeted by sport fishermen. They filled fish boxes just about anywhere along the east coast and the Gulf of Mexico. When commercial fishermen began targeting dolphin, anglers and biologists alike began voicing concern over the possibility of overfishing.

In 2002 the South Carolina Department of Natural Resources launched a highly successful tagging study, aimed at not only showing migration patterns, but establishing a geographic range off the east coast of the United States.

Fisheries managers were amazed at what they found. For the first time, a link was found between the U.S. eastern edge of The Bahamas and fish off the eastern seaboard. Today the research is conducted by a private company that relies on donations to fund this important work. Some of the program's sponsors are listed below.

Marine Ventures Foundation, Jackson Hole, WY
Charleston Fifty – Fifty Tournament, Charleston, SC
South Carolina Department of Natural Resources, Charleston, SC
Harry Hampton Memorial Wildlife Fund, Columbia, SC
Grady-White Boats, Inc., Greenville, NC
Central Florida Offshore Anglers, Orlando, FL
Six Mile Creek, LLC, Charleston, SC
Hilton Head Reef Foundation, Hilton Head, SC

Getting with the Program

Dolphin are not considered overfished by the U.S. federal government which means the private sector has to take responsibility for their well-being. Anglers wanting to get involved with the program can get on board by visiting www.dolphintagging.com.

Imagine trying to get our fathers' generation to tag and release something that tastes like a dolphin. Today's anglers carry a conservation ethic yesterday's anglers never knew was necessary.

Unlike billfish, anglers should not try to tag small dolphin while they're in the water, or dangling from a hook. It's far too easy to lose the tag from the applicator before the fish is under control. You'll be far better off to wet a towel and the deck. Lay the dolphin on the wet deck with one man holding it down with a wet towel over its head. Measure dolphin to center of forked tail and place the tag in the dolphin's shoulder muscle. SB

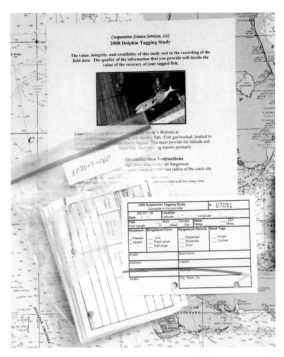

Anglers can get free tagging kits to help in the study (above). That's one lucky dolphin about to swim off with her jewelry in place (below).

CHAPTER 4

Understanding Feeding Behavior

Chicken bones, a rubber monkey, seaweed, sea horses, poptops off a beer can and mantis shrimp are all on the list of weird things that have been found in a dolphin's stomach. None of these we recommend for use as bait, but a hungry dolphin will eat almost anything it can swallow. Then again, the same fish may turn down a live flyingfish an hour later. Because dolphin can be so voracious, many a bluewater fisherman believes that dolphin fishing is easy. "Just get something in front of him and a dolphin will eat anything he can catch and swallow," he'll say. Such is the belief of a man with an empty fish box.

Fact is, a dolphin will turn up its nose at a bait that doesn't swim correctly, or one that looks like something not presently available. "Matching the hatch" isn't just a must for fly fishermen targeting finicky rainbow trout. Your presentations must be accurate, lest your fishing trip turn into a boat ride.

"Just get something in front of him, and he'll eat it. A dolphin will eat anything he can catch and swallow." Such are the beliefs of a man with an empty fish box.

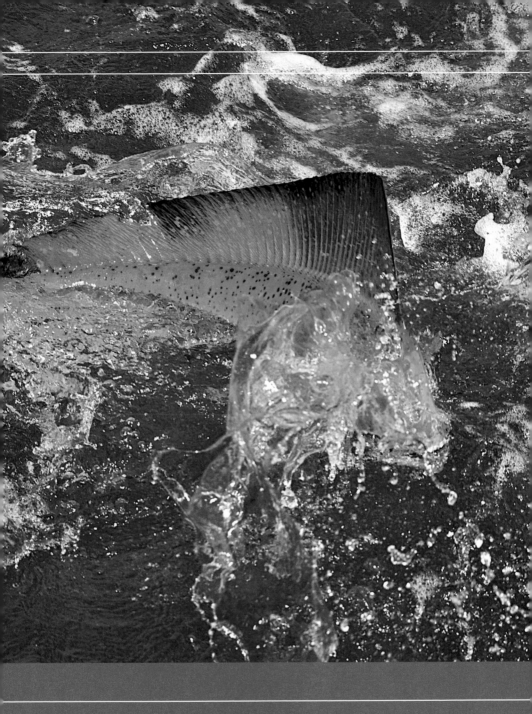

A sight dolphin
anglers live for.
A lit-up dolphin
closes in on his
last meal.

Green Eating Machines

Dolphin are born hungry. Their earliest meals usually consist of the tiniest copepods, which appear almost like dust in the water. Soon dolphin graduate to larger crustaceans and it seems that nothing that wiggles is immune to the attack of the tiny, green eating machines. Within months, no ballyhoo, flyingfish, squid or crab is safe.

Dolphin do the vast majority of their feeding within the first 100 feet of the surface. They are mostly daytime feeders, although swordfish enthusiasts have reported catching hungry dolphin that fell for baits in their spreader lights.

If you look at the physical makeup of a dolphin, it is easy to understand why they spend so much time feeding at the surface. The long, slender, tapered body is specialized for swimming at high speeds. It has pigmented pelvic fins and bands of pigment laterally on both the body and median fins. There is a square supraorbital region, and the dorsal fin runs nearly to the bright yellow caudal fin. They're built for speed and may well light up when feeding to encourage prey into a chase.

The size and location of the eyes explain why the fish feeds where and when it does. Nothing can chase a flyingfish like a dolphin. Think about a wahoo or tuna, with its big eyes high on its head. For that fish to look for food within the first few inches of the surface, it has to look up at a sunny sky. Imagine trying to

chase a hopping ballyhoo without sunglasses or eyelids, by looking straight up into a tropical sky. Dolphin, however, are built with small eyes on the sides of their heads. They can rush a bait with their forehead breaking the surface, looking straight out at their prey. One of the most beautiful sights in nature is watching a flyingfish sailing downwind

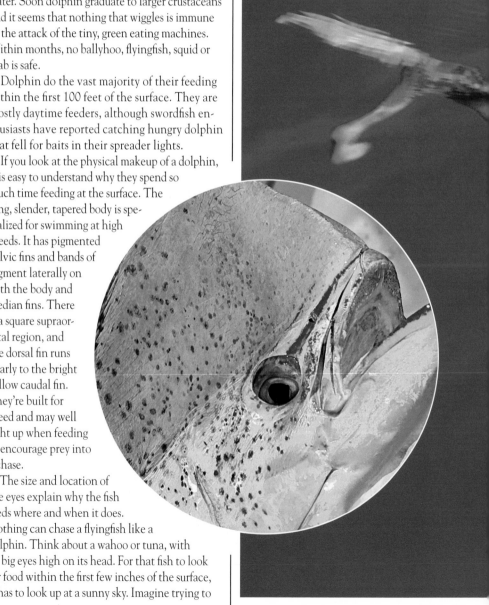

with a yellow-and-green streak following every inch of the way just waiting for splashdown. Take a cue from that behavior, when you scrutinize your spread, and make sure at least a few of those baits are skipping.

You can also get insight into which baits or lures you should pull by checking the stomach contents of your catch. Stomach contents of recent catches can be invaluable to learning feeding behavior. You'll likely find more flyingfish than anything else. This indicates surface feeding. Squid may mean dolphin are feeding deeper or on full-moon nights. Crustaceans or triggerfish mean they're dialed into a weedline, or some other floating object

Eating up to 20 percent of their weight every day means dolphin are hungry most of the time.

The longer something floats, and the more life it has around it, the greater the chances dolphin are hanging nearby.

that's holding food in an area where food may be hard to find. By the way, if there's a young angler or novice angler in your life, showing them the pieces of sargassum and the critters that live in it is a great way to pique their interest in marine life.

Whether dolphin love shade, or the food that seeks the shelter of shade in an open ocean, or both, is unknown. Dolphin of all sizes hang around weedlines, boards and almost whatever else they can find floating at sea. The longer something floats, and the more life it has around it, the greater the chances are that dolphin are hanging nearby. Schoolies generally orient more toward structure than large fish do, which explains why you find clumps of sargassum in their stomachs, along with shrimp, fish, crabs and sea horses. Once located, they're a blast on light tackle. Small cut- or live baits, plugs, crustacean-imitating soft plastics and small flies and jigs work best once you locate a school. In clumps of weeds or around structure, schoolie dolphin are almost always feeding on small prey.

Experienced anglers know better than to draw absolutes when it comes to dolphin behavior. These opportunistic fish can chase a school of flyers forever, or they can spend days slowly cruising under a floating pallet, often turning sideways and plucking filefish directly off the wood. Many anglers think feeding dolphin always prefer hanging on weedlines or under flotsam. Experience says otherwise. Countless times I've trolled a weedline for hours, only to

The Hungry Dolphin

Myriad environmental factors play into dolphin feeding behavior and we'll get into those in another chapter. There are a few truths that have held concerning hungry dolphin over the years:

■ Dolphin feed better when they can see better. They spend most of their lives in clear blue water, and tend to feed better on fair sunny days. Super-slick conditions aren't good; dolphin are more aggressive with a small but manageable sea. Of course, it is much easier to manage baits and lures in a moderate sea, which influences angling success.

■ A dolphin will eat as big a meal as it can swallow. Lure fishermen take note: If you want to target big dolphin, get away from little ballyhoo and small jetheads. Most 50-pound-plus dolphin catches hit either a big swimming mullet, horse ballyhoo or a lure too big for schoolies to handle.

■ Dolphin feed by smell, as well as sight. Dolphin love squid, trolled or cast. It's a good idea to stuff some of the artificial scent baits into rubber squid. The next time you see a dolphin swimming around your boat turning its nose up at a nearly washed-out ballyhoo, grab a fresh squid out of the cooler. Watch how fast the fish jumps it. Calamari tickles its nostrils.

With his fins flared, and his big forehead, this bull's hard to pull against.

A school of tiny fish huddles under sargassum. No doubt keeping an eye out for dolphin.

Different-colored dolphin will mean different moods in the same school.

pull away and start picking off big fish a half-mile from the weeds.

Billfish and dolphin share many similarities in feeding behavior. Raise one billfish, and it may or may not eat. Let a second fish show up, and it's usually "game on." When you find a board with a 40-pound bull holding next to it, he may just refuse whatever you're offering. If his girlfriend shows up and shows an interest, he's bound to charge the bait. They're encouraged by competition. **SB**

Every dolphin fisherman's dream: a floating pallet.

CHAPTER 5

Rigging Your Ride

Everything from johnboats to mega-yachts join the weedline parade, and at different times they may all be successful. However, size matters, especially in rough seas or during long runs.

Your dolphin boat needs the attributes of an NFL linebacker: solid, tall and fast. A sturdy vessel makes long runs through seas smoother, and provides a more stable fishing platform. Height also makes a tremendous difference. You see things at least 10 times farther away from a tuna tower than the rest of the crew can from the deck. Plus, being able to look down on your spread is tremendously helpful because you can readily assess whether baits are swimming inline or fouled. Reaction time to strikes is also cut down. The captain can often see lit-up fish swarm the spread before the bite occurs.

Your dolphin boat needs the attributes of a NFL linebacker: solid, tall and fast. A sturdy vessel makes the run through seas smoother and provides a more stable platform.

DOLPHIN See DVD for more on rigging your boat for dolphin fishing.

Busy days on the rip mean
everything from 18- to 60-
footers will join the parade.

Tricked Out

I f you're serious about catching dolphin, put a great deal of thought and research into buying the right vessel for your fishing and other needs. Dolphin specialists run boats that range from 21-foot center consoles up to 70-foot or larger sportfishers. The smaller boats, up to 39 feet, are primarily center consoles with ample freeboard and a sharp deadrise to break through waves. If you plan on running and gunning, a bigger boat with sharper deadrise makes it more comfortable. If trolling is your primary game, look for a boat that is economical to run and allows for a wide spread of baits.

Cuddy cabins or express models give you more comfort, but center consoles let you fish 360 degrees.

Families often prefer "pocket sport fishermen" where you can get out of the weather.

while offshore, because the person will quickly become sick and tired.

Sportfishers, the luxury liners of offshore fishing, run from 35 feet on up to colossal custom yachts.

Boat options include factory models, semi-custom craft, and custom-made center consoles and sportfishers. Most center consoles are rigged with outboard power. One or more inboard diesels is another option for center consoles, cuddy cabins and express models. There's a growing list of inboard/outboard models out there, too. Most sportfishers have inboard

Cuddy cabins or express models offer a small forward cabin and storage area, and usually a head. These boats range in size from about 23 to 44 feet. They're great for families in calm seas. But, do not let anyone who says "I'm tired" go down below

Outboard power usually means a bigger cockpit. Center consoles allow 360-degree battles (below).

engines, primarily diesel-powered. But some manufacturers are going the outboard route for smaller sportfishers. As you decide on a boat, think about how you would rig it, in terms of its layout and fishability.

Fishability

Good dolphin fishermen cast to as many dolphin as they troll up. Often, there isn't time to square the stern up for a cast. All sight fishing requires 360-degree fishability, and in this game, center consoles have a distinct advantage. Make sure your anglers can run around the boat and fire a cast from any angle. Kite fishing gets more popular every year, and many a reluctant big bull has fallen to a kicking goggle-eye flown from a kite. Big center consoles are easy places to

launch a kite from. Rod holders spread around 360 degrees are mandatory for good dolphin fishing on center consoles.

Above, keeping your terminal tackle nearby and organized is a must. Below, rocket launchers keep rods at the ready and out of the way.

Leaning Post and Command Center

Dolphin fishing usually goes from slow to bedlam in a split second. Therefore, you've got to have a clean deck and orderly command station. When you shop around for a boat, look for a model that offers the most tackle boxes in small built-in compartments, a leaning post or the rocket launcher. In the heat of the battle against a school of dolphin, you want to be able to stick the fish in the box, cut the line and tie on a new hook

There's no such thing as too many rod holders or too much tackle storage.

quickly. Dolphin do not hang around indefinitely.

Few fish are more dangerous in a boat than a large dolphin. They are as flexible as snakes, and can strike like a rattler with the tail. The best way to handle a dolphin is to bail or gaff the fish and throw it immediately into an in-deck fish box. A good dolphin boat offers at least one 5-foot or larger in-deck fish box. In lieu of a fish box, a 100-plus-quart cooler will do, but can get in the way. A bait cooler is another necessity. Boats with room to shove the bait cooler under the gunnels or leaning post keep one more thing out of the way while you're fighting a fish on a slick, bloody deck.

Towers

All boats are not built for towers, and all towers are not built for all boats. A 2-foot wave can roll a boat because of too much weight up in the tower. The rule of thumb is that the space between the hardtop and the floor of the tower should be about 12 percent of the length of the boat. On a 35-foot boat, for instance, you want about four feet between the hardtop and tower; eight or nine feet on a 70-footer.

Keeping safety in mind, understand that the higher off the deck you can get in the search

Many center consoles now sport mini towers. The higher you get, the better you see.

of weedlines and other floating objects, the farther you can see. Customizing your tower also helps your game.

Most people opt for a sun shade on the tower, but there is a tradeoff to keeping your noggin cool. You lose a little visibility and the ability to scan 360 degrees, plus you lose the chance to cast to swimming fish.

Many towers are designed more with safety in mind than fishing functionality. In many towers, the backrest is too high, which keeps you from falling out. But if it's higher than your waist it blocks your vision of the baits and cockpit. You want a backrest that comes to no more than waist high. The most important thing a tower can give you is 360-degree visibility.

Power controls on the tower are an important investment. If you don't have controls on the tower, you just added the necessity of one more crew member to run the boat down below. Down low, the driver can't watch for fish and run the boat, so a boat without tower controls is much less effective. Plus, there is the time lost in translation between the man in the tower and the man on the controls.

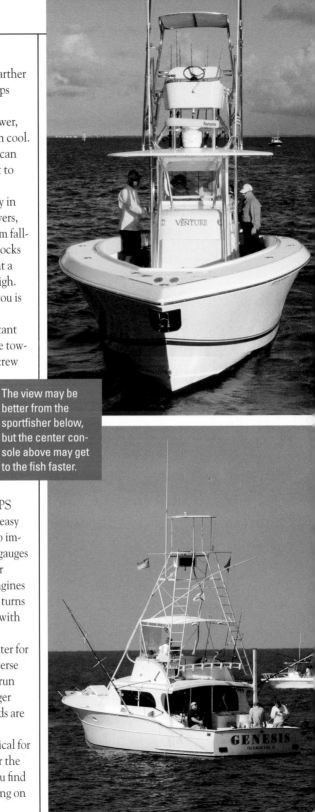

The view may be better from the sportfisher below, but the center console above may get to the fish faster.

When you trick out your tower, be careful to put the bottom machine and GPS (usually one unit these days) where they are easy to read—in the shade. Engine gauges are also important. If no one is paying attention to the gauges below, you can overheat an engine and never realize it, until it's too late. (Most modern engines have some over-heating fail-safe device that turns the engine off before damage occurs. Not so with older models.)

The more rod holders on the boat, the better for dolphin fishing. Even on the tower, have diverse rigs ready and backups handy. Some anglers run a shotgun line out of the tower. A center rigger out of the tower is standard, but often the rods are downstairs.

If a tower isn't in your budget or not practical for your boat, try standing on a secured cooler or the gunnel in calm seas. These positions help you find weeds or flotsam that you may not see standing on the deck.

Having matching screens like these two Raymarine 12-inch units means you can watch several functions at once.

Electronics

A sonar fishfinder and Global Positioning System (GPS) unit are helpful, whether installed separately or, more common these days, in a single combination unit. When the current hits sizeable bottom structure it creates a surface structure called a rip. Generally, rips line up along sharper contours on the continental shelf. In Southeast Florida, the tidal influence from inlets bucking the Gulf Stream also creates rips. Ideally, you want to be able to read depths, locate special bottom contours and identify bait schools. A sea-surface temperature indicator is also essential, given the dolphin's relatively narrow temperature range tolerances.

A GPS is really handy when you lose track of fish movements. By using the chartplotter feature, you can at least tell where you've been and the general direction the fish were headed. Within the last three years, satellite imagery has started appearing on the better electronic packages. And it's changing everything. If you order satellite weather from Sirius or other services you get up-to-the-minute sea-surface temperature charts, every time the satellite takes a picture. My experience with such data? I've run 20 miles out of my way to find a temperature break, and found it within a hundred feet of where the satellite picture said it would be. You also know where thunderstorms are mushrooming and have plenty of notice to avoid them. Anglers can also find recent satellite pictures at a number of sites on the Internet.

The ability to hit the Man Overboard (MOB) button, giving you coordinates to return to the spot where you encountered fish or structure, is also extremely helpful. With the speed at which dolphin travel, a barren board at 7 a.m. might become a day-saver at 3 p.m.

> **The availability to hit the Man Overboard (MOB) button means you can return to your last strike.**

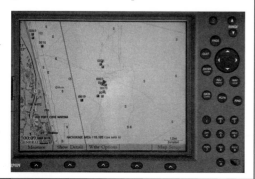

Radar

Radar has proven an invaluable fish-finding tool, because you can tell the difference between solid objects on the screen and flocks of birds. Tuna fishermen were the first to use radar to spot big flocks, but skilled dolphin fishermen soon learned the difference between spotting a big flock of birds over a school of tuna and spotting a couple frigate birds holding over a traveling school of dolphin. The light marks of a few traveling frigates can usually only be spotted by higher-wattage, open-array radars. Better to save money on the fancy paint job, and invest in the best radar you can find.

Open-array radar is far superior to a dome. These are the systems you see where the bar goes around in a circle. The open array is far more sensitive, helping you to spot and identify birds. (Functionally, the higher the kilowatts or wattage, the more detailed picture you get.) Unfortunately, open-array radar is also a massive power drain. You will quickly kill your battery powering an open-array off an outboard motor with a single battery unless the boat is running. Open-array systems are commonly 4 kW, 7 kW, 12 kW or 25 kW. Domes, 4 kW or less. You can run up to a 12 kW unit, but the usual choice for recreational fishing vessels is a 4- or 7-kW array with a standard two-battery setup on a center console boat. The weight of the unit may not allow you to put an open-array system on a smaller boat. Open-array systems weigh 60 pounds and most T-tops are not certified to take that kind of weight in a pounding sea.

ON THE RADAR
Some maintain that exposure to radar microwaves can cause cancer and a loss of virility. That's a bit of a wives' tale. But you should never stare at an open array radar at less than three feet, because it can damage your eyes. It's probably a good idea to limit a kid's exposure, just in case.

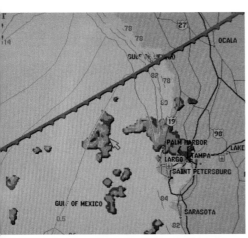

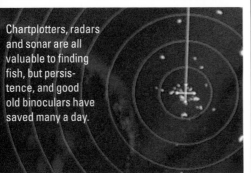

Chartplotters, radars and sonar are all valuable to finding fish, but persistence, and good old binoculars have saved many a day.

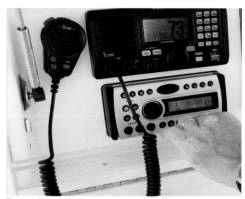

Forget the tunes, I want to hear the other boats chatter.

Handheld radios are best used as backups.

Marine Radio

You want to buy as good a VHF (Very High Frequency) radio and as sensitive an antenna as you can afford. Offshore, a radio is your lifeline to the world in a dicey situation, and it's also a handy tool for eavesdropping on fishing reports. If an overzealous weekender spills the beans on a rip 20 miles away, you want to be the one who hears him first.

Radios are available in both fixed-mount and hand-held models. All fixed-mount VHFs have a maximum output of 25 watts, the maximum allowed by the Federal Communications Commission (FCC). Note that VHF is a line-of-sight system, which means the radio waves won't bend to follow the curvature of the earth. The VHF antenna must "see" the antenna of a distant station. Therefore, antenna height is more important in determining range than radio wattage. The effective useful range of a fix-mounted VHF radio is 20 to 25 miles.

Just because the radio generates a 25-watt

Livewells

Livewells have evolved substantially over the past few decades. We started with 5-gallon buckets with an aerator and now have luxury spas for baits that include running water, curved corners—so that baits don't constantly bump corners and get red noses—and lights. Multiple baitwells allow you to segregate bait by species.

An above-the-floor livewell is perhaps the most convenient, and offers quick access to pitch baits when you see big dolphin swim under the boat. Large wells are great for carrying many dozens of baits. But give a good angler a smaller well with great circulation, and a couple of blue runners grabbed from under a buoy on the way out, and he'll have your 40-pounder on ice while you're still catching bait.

This angler is carrying enough bait to last all day. Will it be fresh enough at 4 p.m.? Clear lid lets you check their condition.

signal, the net power out the end of the antenna is likely to be less than 25 watts unless you have a professional tune your fixed-mount antenna. The difference is made in the wires and connectors. A technician can improve the connections and coat the wires with silver or gold plating, minerals that are superior conductors, so that the signal comes out at 25 watts from the end of the antenna.

Handheld VHF radios also offer many of the same features found on fixed-mount units. They offer portability and may be just what you need for use in a smaller boat without electrical systems, or as an emergency backup for your boat's radio. As of this writing, handhelds have a maximum output of six watts. However, VHF technology improves every year. The short antenna is also a limiting factor in range. A significant increase in range can be achieved by connecting an external antenna or using a telescoping antenna mounted to the handheld radio. Battery life varies. Some have battery saver circuits that turn off the receiver to save power. The battery life of a handheld can be increased by switching from full transmit power to one watt of transmit power.

Digital Selective Calling, or DSC, is the equivalent of a "mayday button" on a VHF. When activated, it automatically broadcasts an encoded distress call that will be picked up by all nearby vessels equipped with DSC. If the radio is interfaced with a Loran or GPS, it will also automatically broadcast the distressed vessel's position. DSC is also a way to talk privately with a specific boat. It transmits on VHF Channel 70, but only transmits on one watt, and the range is very limited. To use DSC, you must obtain a Maritime Mobile Service Identity (MMSI) number.

The FCC regulates marine radio traffic and dictates that all other uses are secondary to safety, so chatting is frowned upon by the FCC and forbidden on channels 16 and 9.

Cell phones can be equipped with amplifiers, which actually just takes us back to the range of the old analog bag phones. Thirty miles at sea seems to be about the limit. **SB**

Outriggers

Pin adjustments are vital and should be determined by the size bait.

Outriggers are more essential when you're not sure where the fish are. If you're trolling without outriggers all your baits are clumped in a column only as wide as your transom. But with a pair of 25-foot outriggers you're cutting a path through the water more than 60 feet wide. The baits and teasers are in clear water outside the wake. When you get a bite the first few seconds of dropback are automatic.

When using outriggers, the line goes out through clips, which need to be set at a tension according to the lure or bait you're pulling. A big lure needs a heavy setting, but a naked ballyhoo needs a relatively light setting. Transom-mount flatline clips are also a good idea, as the bait will track straighter. They're especially handy when slow-trolling live baits, which tend to swim across other lines.

A downrigger can get in the way, but many anglers swear by slow-trolling a live bait down 30 to 50 feet during the heat of the day. You can also drag a plug or spoon on a downrigger while trolling, which may attract wahoo as well as dolphin. Planers can be used to drag plugs or spoons deeper in the water column.

CHAPTER 6

Balancing Your Tackle

Having balanced tackle is important when fishing for dolphin. You're going to need a few different types of outfits. You need rods capable of putting enough pressure on a 40-pound bull to turn his head, and you'd better have one capable of launching a live sardine far enough to tempt a fish that keeps shying away from the boat.

Just about every fishing tackle retailer sells what they call "balanced combos," meaning that the rod, reel and line are in proportion to each other. You can also custom-match rods and reels. Choosing the right line and minimizing terminal tackle are equally important considerations.

Even though the plan may be to let the grandkids catch a few schoolies, you need to remember that anywhere there are schoolies there is the potential for the fish of a lifetime to show up. Make sure you're prepared for that bull.

Rods, reels, line, leaders, swivels, weights and hooks all have to be in balance to make a great presentation. Have one piece out of balance, and you'll be less effective.

DOLPHIN

See DVD for more on balancing your tackle.

Having conventional tackle, spinners, plugs and jigs all at the ready (above) pays off with a nice gaffer (right).

Rods & Reels

Fast-trolling a small lure past a floating object pays off with a nice schoolie.

To determine what you need for rods and reels, visualize how you plan to spend the day.

Balanced tackle starts at the butt of the rod and ends at the point of the hook. To determine what you need for rod and reels, you have to visualize how you plan to spend the day. For trolling, make sure your sticks are stout enough. You can troll with medium to light spinners, or small conventional reels on light trolling rods. Light tackle poses several problems. If you're going to troll with ballyhoo or small trolling lures, it takes a rod with some backbone to ensure the hook penetrates the jaw of a big bull. Using soft-tipped rods and light drags is a great idea with super-sharp, small livebait hooks—especially circle hooks—but driving home a 9/0 stainless steel trolling hook and keeping it stuck requires more stick.

You'll want to take your crew into consideration before deciding what outfits to take with you. Tiagra 50s or Penn 6/0s will whip a big dolphin quickly, but they're often too heavy for some people to enjoy. Oftentimes, rookies have a harder time with spinning gear, and can't grasp the concept of only reeling when you can gain line. In both these situations some of the newer 6:1 retrieve ratio light conventional reels are golden. Matching the rod and reel to your angler is just as important as matching it to your target fish.

For decades most charterboats have always erred on the side of heavy tackle, thinking the end result of a full fish box was the mark of a good day.

Today's smart captains, whether charter or private, have learned that their crew having a great time is the true mark of a good day. This can often be accomplished by using tackle that matches their ability as well as their target.

Big center consoles have the advantage of almost endless rod holders. Having several rods ready to troll or cast means you'll be able to get a bait in front of a dolphin as soon as you find him.

Conventional Trolling Tackle

I can still remember the old Ocean City reel my dad got us for many books of S+H Green Stamps. It weighed at least 5 pounds, and had big-game features like a one-to-one gear ratio and direct drive. That meant every time you turned the reel handle one time, the spool went around one time. If the fish took off you'd better be ready, as the handle was about to bruise your knuckles. We never hooked a really big king or a wahoo on it. Come to think of it, I think I'm glad we didn't.

Years later we evolved to leather drag washers. They really worked pretty well, at least until they got wet. Here's a thought. Fishing with tackle that has to stay dry is probably not going to work out very well.

Now, the gear ratios are often six-to-one, expressed as 6:1. The graphite drags are so smooth, you can't even feel the line coming off the reels. Just think about how many fish sticky drags have cost fishermen. For years I thought fish started and stopped several runs during a fight. It wasn't the fish, it was the drag that started and stopped.

Ideal Dolphin Setup:
- ▶ Leverdrag 4/0 reel
- ▶ 6½ foot fiberglass rod with roller tip and gimbal butt
- ▶ 600-plus yards 30 lb. mono

Conventional Trolling Rods

For rods, I've run the whole gamut from 5½ to 7½ feet, and for my crew, 6½ feet seems to be right. I've also gone from fiberglass to graphite, and back. There's a lot more sensitivity in the new generation fiberglass, or "e-glass," without the occasional "snap" of breaking graphite. I used to be a nut for roller guides, but the eyes made from aluminum oxide, or silicon carbide, are extremely smooth and more than adequate. A gimbal is nice for locking in position in the rod holder, but will require you to use a belt or a gimbal cover if you hook up with a big fish.

Serious tackle means no schoolies for this crew.

Conventional Reels

Today's dolphin anglers are clearly shopping in the best of times for tackle buyers. A few of the things you'll need to decide on are line capacity, gear ratio, whether or not to have a levelwind, and leverdrag versus star drag.

Levelwind reel okay for small fish, new anglers.

Penn Special Senator 114H, a proven star-drag reel.

Smooth leverdrags are best for big dolphin.

Levelwind Reels

If you're just starting your offshore experience, you may be tempted to carry the convenience of the levelwind on your baitcaster onto your trolling reels. In a word, don't. I've never seen a levelwind that could keep up with a rampaging dolphin. You're going to have to learn to keep your line packed on the reel evenly by steering it back and forth with your thumb as you retrieve.

Star vs. Leverdrag

I was raised on star-drag reels, and I still love them for bottom fishing. For dolphin, I'm a convert to leverdrags. You can troll with a light drag to enable the fish to get the bait in its mouth better, and then turn up the heat during the fight, all the while able to see how much pressure you're applying by looking at where the lever is.

Two-Speed Reels

Two-speed reels are a whole new level for the hardcore angler. Down-shifting from 4:1 to 1.5:1 can really turn up the pressure on a fish, but I haven't found this feature necessary on very many dolphin. To be honest, we've probably downshifted more often to reel in large clumps of weeds, than we have to battle dolphin.

Line Capacity

You want at least 300 yards of line capacity. I've never had my reel stripped by a dolphin, but I've sure come close. Open boats can stay closer to their fish than classic flybridge boats by putting their anglers on the bow, but be aware that double hookups of big dolphin have a habit of taking off in opposite directions. You'll need to have enough line to stay with both of them.

Spinning Tackle

Does life ever get better than when you match a young crew against a batch of schoolies on light spinning tackle?

Spinning outfits have some advantages over conventional reels, but they also have some definite drawbacks.

The ability to launch a small jig, chunk of ballyhoo or a 6-inch sardine means spinning reels are required on any true dolphin hunter's boat. Veteran South Florida skipper Bouncer Smith says more than half his dolphin are spotted before they're caught.

That means being able to cast great distances with something as light as a chunk of ballyhoo. The bottom line on running and gunning for dolphin is, if you can't cast, you can't play. The biggest baitcasters can be used to cast at dolphin, but unless you're a real expert, spinners are far easier to cast.

Left-handed anglers are certainly appreciative of being able to switch the spinner's handle from side

Ideal Dolphin Spin Setup:

► (2) 20 lb. reels on 7-foot fiberglass rods with 20 lb. mono (300 yards or 30 lb. braid and 200 yards 20 lb. mono backing)

► (2) 15 lb. reels on 7-foot fiberglass rods with 12-15 lb. mono (200 yards or 20 lb. braid and 150 yards 15 lb. mono backing)

to side. Anglers working toward setting records, whether personal or IGFA, find it plenty helpful to be able to pop off one spool and put on another.

When you're talking bluewater fish, spinners are better suited to chasing dolphin than any fish that swims. Not only is the ability to cast vital, but being able to release

Today's spinning outfits can handle even the biggest dolphin.

the bail, and let a live bait run free, is often just the provocation a big bull needs to crush your live bait. This can also be accomplished by using the "bait runner" feature some of the new spinners possess.

The first and perhaps biggest drawback to spinners is line capacity. The biggest spinner around can't touch the line capacity of a 30-pound conventional reel. Braided polyethylene line is certainly a boost to the line capacity of spinners. But by the time you put your line up to a kite, and down to the surface, you've taken half the line off most spinners.

My experience has been it's easier for most people to fight a big fish on conventional trolling reels than on spinners. An inexperienced angler can crank on a conventional reel while his fish is peeling drag off without twisting the line. Try turning the handle on a spinner without retrieving line. You're about one second of slack away from twisted line wrapping around the tip of your rod, kissing your big fish goodbye.

You can troll for wahoo with your 30-pound conventional reels, or

you can jig for grouper with your spinners, but if dolphin are your target, you better have both types at the ready.

Dolphin Come in All Sizes

If you're smart, you'll have a couple different-size spinners, based on your anglers' ages and abilities. When teaching juniors to fish, it's important to match their size with a typical 12-pound-test spinner on a light rod. Your typical schoolie (3 to 8 pounds) can be the fish of a lifetime matched up with the correct tackle.

Terminal Tackle

Select hooks, leaders, swivels and lure size with the breaking strength of your line in mind. You can't set a 12/0 hook with 20-pound test; you'll pull out little livebait hooks with 50-pound test. And whether you're fishing for the biggest, smartest bream in the pond or a record dolphin, you'll get more bites when you learn to minimize the amount of terminal tackle you put in the water.

Keep in mind that baits will look more natural when they're not overburdened with unnecessarily heavy leaders and hooks. Why use an 80-pound swivel or a 200-pound leader when your main line breaks at 20 pounds of pull?

Long wind-on leaders are helpful; otherwise snap swivels can get stuck in the top rod eye or the mate has to drag the fish into gaffing range, which risks snapping the fish off or throwing enough slack into the line for the fish to throw the hook. You can either buy wind-on leaders premade, or whip up a Bimini twist and then tie on 15 feet of 100-pound mono with a Yucatan or other line-to-line knot. When a big dolphin is finally wrestled close, you want the mate to be able to crank up the pressure to speed

Hook this bull while high-speed trolling, and you'll be glad your hook is not only big enough but has a thick diameter.

up the end game. If it's a fish headed for the box, you want to get it under control for the gaff man. If the fish is to be released, the sooner you can free it the better its chances for survival.

Hooks

Today's anglers have the option of fishing with hooks sharp enough to drive right through the toughest jaw in the ocean. Modern hook technology has made hook sharpeners less and less necessary. Whether they're sharpened with a laser, or ground to a fine point, today's hooks come out of the package sharper than the best mate could have hoped to sharpen them 20 years ago.

There are several things to consider before deciding which hooks to use in what situation. Think of the size of your tackle, the bait you're using, and the speed you're trolling. Always keep in mind, hooks don't bend or break under normal circumstances. If you straighten out one of today's new breed of hooks, chances are you had too much pressure on a hook not designed to take it.

Hook wire diameter is just as important as hook size. For example, let's talk about a Mustad 9174 shortshank 6/0. It's a great hook for rigging small ballyhoo. You could pull a truck up a hill without straightening it out, but if you put it through the nostrils of a sardine, it'll be dead in no time.

Conversely, a VMC 7198 5/0 livebait hook is as sharp as they come and offset to help hold it in place. It's thin diameter means your nostril-hooked live bait can swim for hours. The

problem is, that same thin diameter means it will rip through a fish's mouth, or straighten out under a heavy load.

Offset hooks are deadly for either live bait or drifted chunks. Place a flat hook between two pieces of cardboard. Pull on it and it will slide right out. Try the same trick with an offset hook, and

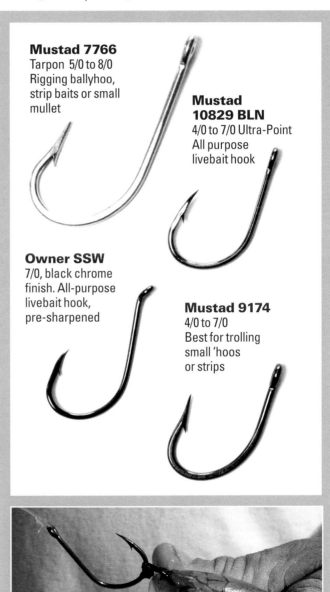

Mustad 7766
Tarpon 5/0 to 8/0
Rigging ballyhoo, strip baits or small mullet

Mustad 10829 BLN
4/0 to 7/0 Ultra-Point
All purpose livebait hook

Owner SSW
7/0, black chrome finish. All-purpose livebait hook, pre-sharpened

Mustad 9174
4/0 to 7/0
Best for trolling small 'hoos or strips

Live baits usually swim best when bridled to a livebait hook.

Buying your hooks in small, sealed bags will do a better job of keeping them rust free until they hit the water.

Swivels

You'll want a swivel in most situations. Selecting the proper swivel requires the use of common sense. Consider this example: Decades ago, a dear friend of mine set out to fulfill a lifelong goal of catching a blue marlin off the coast of Northeast Florida. He had old Penn Senator 10/0 reels spooled with 80-pound-test Dacron, each rigged with Spanish mackerel sewn on 12/0 hooks. He had a belt and harness at the ready. Sure enough, after miles and miles of watching his baits and teasers, he saw a big blue pop up right behind the teaser. My buddy dropped a Spanish right down the big girl's mouth. Unfortunately, he had the whole rig put together with a 40-pound snap swivel. End of story.

you'll understand why they work so well. I once decided that going to offset hooks would greatly increase my hookup ratio on ballyhoo. I made up 100 rigs and carefully rigged four dozen ballyhoo the night before a sailfish tournament. Let me save you from that particular debacle. If you try trolling ballyhoo with a hook that's offset even 10 percent, you'll end up with a bunch of helicopters following your boat.

I always upsize my hooks when our trolling speed increases. Believe me, if a big dolphin hits your lure at 12 knots, you'll be thankful it's connected to a hook able to handle the weight and not pull through the fish's mouth.

In my tackle box I try to stay stocked on 4/0 and 6/0 offset livebait hooks. My small ballyhoo are rigged on shortshank 7/0; my medium ballyhoo usually a standard 8/0 needle eye. I've had the best success with my large ballyhoo pulling them on a standard shank 10/0. Everybody has their favorites, but the light weight and consistent sharpness of the VMC 9255 ballyhoo hooks have long been a favorite of mine. For my big lures, the VMC 8705 Dyna Cut hooks have worked out well.

Stainless steel swivels allow you to use smaller sizes.

Always spend a little extra for ball-bearing snap swivels.

Quality ball-bearing snap swivel and crimp to wind-on leader.

Leaders

Mono leaders are your best choice. Just remember to check them often for nicks.

I still own a spool of 105-pound wire leader, but I'll bet it won't be empty anytime soon. I've gone to mono for 90 percent of my trolling; no wonder it seems I use less wire every year.

The fact is, I get many more bites and a better hookup ratio with mono. I more than make up for the occasional bite-off by a toothy critter. (For my swimming plugs, I'll still use wire to increase their wobble.)

Mono leaders get more bites, and a better hookup ratio.

If you check the stomach contents of the dolphin you clean, you'll notice almost all their food is swallowed head first. That means when they attack from behind they have to turn the bait to swallow it. That's got to be considerably harder on a piece of wire.

Mono allows your baits to swim naturally in the water, is easier to rig with, and gets you more bites and better hookup ratios. Of course we lose some toothy fish to bite-offs, but we get so many more wahoo bites, the difference is minimal. SB

Crimps vs. Knots

For most dolphin fishing, an 80- to 100-pound-test monofilament leader is sufficient. When working with leader under 100 pounds, I have no trouble tying a uni-knot for a connection, or snelling an offset eye on a livebait hook. To this day, I've never had a uni-knot fail.

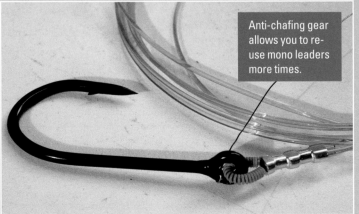

Anti-chafing gear allows you to re-use mono leaders more times.

For high-speed lures that perform best on heavy leaders, crimping is a must. I check every crimp before it hits the water, and invariably one in a thousand or so will fail, because I goofed. Make sure you check yours.

CHAPTER 7

Clues to The Puzzle

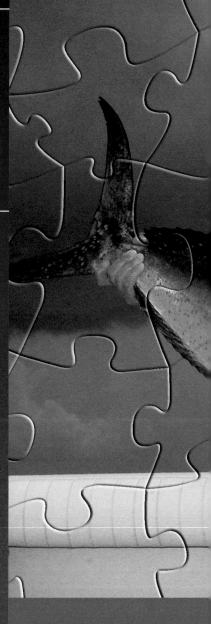

Dolphin don't swim from one good wreck to another like an old grouper. They move with the winds of change, often up to 200 miles per day. But that's also one of the best things about dolphin fishing. Every day presents a new puzzle to figure out.

The puzzle pieces are diverse. Annual migrations, satellite pictures, bait availability, water temp and clarity, wind direction and current velocity all factor in. Throw in some emerging factors for sport fishermen—such as trying to figure out how we can run-and-gun on skyrocketing fuel prices—and the plot thickens. Where's the weedline? Have we had enough storms in the Caribbean to send up some floating trees? Did anybody fish the buoys this morning? Is there a temperature break within reach? Where is it going? Is there enough live bait around to catch, without being the last boat to the rip? These are all questions you need to stab at when planning a trip.

Starting out each day with more questions than answers is one the best parts of dolphin fishing. The questions of where to go and what to do when you get there, start over every day.

Putting together
the puzzle pieces
paid off with this
super slammer.

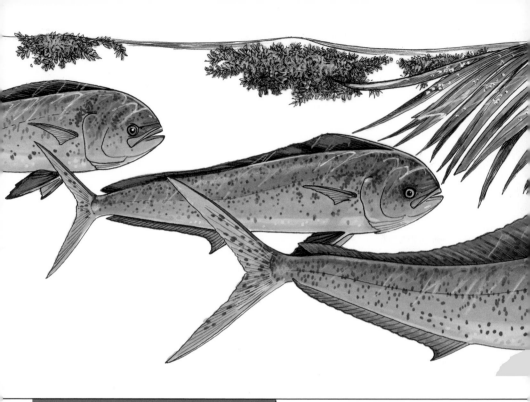

Finding Fish

Many people don't understand the Gulf Stream is a river whose tributaries twist throughout the Gulf of Mexico and Atlantic Ocean.

You don't need to waste precious fishing time and fuel chasing dolphin in water colder than 76 degrees. Dolphin fishing usually isn't all that productive when the winds have been blowing out to sea for days.

On the U.S. East Coast, you want a wind that pushes up the "golden floaters," rips and schools of bait brought into range by the Gulf Stream. Typically, that means an east or southeast breeze.

Odds are, if you bought this book, you will target dolphin in Gulf Stream waters. But many people don't understand that the Gulf Stream is a river whose tributaries and branches loop and twist throughout the Gulf of Mexico and Atlantic Ocean. Eddies and spinoffs sometimes cause the current to back up and run south. The Gulf Stream is the engine that drives migrations, the blanket that keeps northern Atlantic waters warm and the vehicle that brings the conditions dolphin anglers love.

Dolphin aren't structure-oriented in and of themselves, but often relate to bottom structure that holds bait. Dolphin

that shows him where the rips are before he leaves the dock.

Learning the basics of satellite imagery is pretty easy. If you check the computer the night before your trip, you'll be able to see where the sharpest water temperature contrasts exist. At sea, these will usually appear as weedlines or water-color changes visible to the naked eye. Learning how to spot contrasts on your computer gives you more information than most of the weekenders leaving the dock. Just move your cursor over the top of the temperature break and write the lat/lon numbers down.

Have you ever wondered why the same charter-boat that whacked the dolphin southeast of the inlet yesterday just pulled out and headed northeast? It's because the captain has learned to track the

spend most of their time in the upper 100 feet of the water column. Surface "structure," such as a rip, will almost always concentrate them in the greatest numbers. Understand the conditions that bring surface structure.

The most obvious dolphin gathering spots are rips or weedlines. Rips are caused by two currents meeting or a current colliding with a reef ridge or sharp contour on the continental shelf. Usually rips are most easily spotted by the floating objects trapped in line, but floaters are not necessary to ensure success. The intersection of two currents of differing water temps may attract fish without much visible evidence other than a subtle color change.

The collision of two currents usually traps floating weeds, logs and all the junk that humans have put in the ocean. This flotsam and jetsam provide homes for the crustaceans and baitfish that dolphin feed on almost nonstop. These days, rips can be monitored through satellite imagery. You can bet the guy at the ramp who consistently catches more fish than you has a Web site bookmarked on his computer

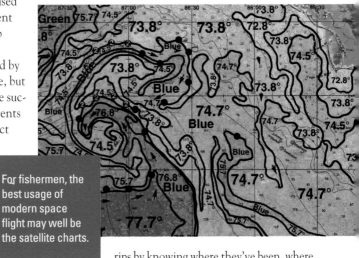

For fishermen, the best usage of modern space flight may well be the satellite charts.

rips by knowing where they've been, where they're headed and whether they're getting stronger or weaker. It's a good idea to check the computer or a commercial e-mail or fax service, such as ROFFS, before the trip to see where to start. It's also helpful to review such imagery after the trip as well, to identify productive zones.

Birds

As discussed in Chapter 5, a good radar system is extremely helpful in locating distant birds. With radar you can spot flocks of terns, even lone frigatebirds, at a range of miles, well beyond the range of the naked eye. At the least, you'll want a pair of weather-resistant binoculars. Always keep an eye out for low-flying birds, which may be tough to discern on radar.

Frigatebirds often lead the way to big bulls. Long and thin, with iridescent black feathers, frigates have a scissor-shaped tail and an impressive wingspan—up to 90 inches. In fact, in Latin America, anglers call them "tijera," the Spanish word for scissors. The distinctive birds dive for food accompanying the debris or weedlines. When a frigate spots fish, it will fly in high, lazy circles over the spot. It will continue circling until the fish come up to feed or go deep. When you see the frigatebird start circling close to the water, make sure you have baits out. The fish are feeding and the frigate is there to pick up the scraps or chase down a tasty flyingfish.

The frigate will sometimes stop circling and fly off in a straight line. This is a good time to pick up lines and follow the bird. Watch the surface under the frigatebird and you may see weeds or other floating objects with smaller terns or other birds working the surface.

You may be led astray by other birds, but a circling frigatebird tells no lies. The frigate has spotted predators and it's up to you to catch them.

Birds circling low to the water is an unmistakable sign.

A sky full of frigates means there's an ocean full of predators below.

Petrels and Terns

Petrels may show the way to success with dolphin as well. However, they may signify skipjack and other tuna rather than dolphin. Experienced captains and veteran anglers determine what species likely lies beneath them by the bird's behavior.

Pelagic terns and small storm petrels—tuna birds or bonito birds, as they are sometimes called—can be seen singly, in large flocks or just three or four birds. A large flock of birds diving into the water or actually sitting on the water and looking down usually means tuna. They could be little tunny, skipjack tuna or blackfin tuna.

When you see these birds singly or in groups of 2 to 10, and they are diving and swooping over patches of weed or a weedline, they are following feeding dolphin. Dolphin feed on the small fish that hide under the sargassum weed and birds swoop in to pick up the scraps or perhaps grab a flyingfish that is being chased by a dolphin. The trick is to get around to the outside of where these birds are working and troll your baits in a circle around them.

Royal tern (top) circles the action. Masked boobies (bottom) sit on a floater, their white plumage visible from afar.

Laughing gull, mainly a near-coastal species, scavenges tidbits left behind by a dolphin school on the feed.

Weedlines

Not all weedlines are created equal. Finding weeds is not enough to ensure a good day. Having weeds to troll around is great, but I've come across rips with nothing but eelgrass in them. Eelgrass will keep your hooks fouled while adding nothing to your fish box.

Secondly, live sargassum (a free-floating algae) is a real plus. Live sargassum is lighter in color than dead weed and is better at holding the most important factor of all, bait. I've never been a big believer in the theory that dolphin love shade. Dolphin are highly mobile eating machines. They'd starve to death languishing under shade. But dolphin love to eat the things that hide in the shade; hence they're often around the weeds. Find

live weeds holding bait and your odds of a full fish box go way up.

Like the cast of characters that ride along with it, the weed itself has quite a story. For decades, scientists believed the weed broke off from the ocean floor and floated to the surface. Now we've learned sargassum spends its entire life adrift. Specialized air bladders that look like clusters of grapes keep the weed afloat. You would expect to find juvenile dolphin, sailfish and wahoo in the weeds, but permit, red porgies,

Live sargassum is the weed you want. Shake it out and it looks like you spilled an aquarium.

Having trolled until they found the spot, it looks like these guys are on fish.

A patch of live sargassum looks like a mini saltwater aquarium through a mask. Dive in and take a look.

flounder and mullet? They've all been found miles at sea, hiding in clumps of sargassum.

Don't underestimate the value of sargassum to the health of the ocean. Once harvested off our coast for livestock feed, sargassum is the nursery for just about every important piece of the aquatic food chain. You can't pick up a piece of live sargassum in the open ocean without finding shrimp, crabs, and numerous fish—both full-time residents and just-hatched future predators.

Long nighttime swordfish drifts have left me plenty of time to dip up sargassum clumps to see who's using it. Scores of newborn dolphin, brand-new wahoo, and numerous others too small to identify have all shown up hiding in the weeds.

Whereas we're all happy when we find a weedline or floating board, it's important to remember to use extreme caution while fishing in the area. Ropes, submerged logs big enough to sink a battleship, hundreds of plastic bags, and even a chained-up refrigerator with a skull and crossbones are all very hazardous

The same dolphin foraging weeds for tiny morsels (above) will readily attack a larger trolling lure (right).

materials I've found in weedlines.

For inboard boats the dangers are worse. Picking up somebody's lost dock line or sucking a plastic bag into your raw-water intake means somebody's going overboard. Always remember to carry a mask and snorkel for emergencies in a weedline.

Rips and Currents

Basically, there are four aspects to determine whether a rip is worth fishing: water color, type and age of weed or debris present, forage abundance and water temperature. As to color, look for two different shades. Dolphin will come in relatively shallow (less than 80 feet), but only in conducive conditions. They prefer clear, blue ocean water. Whether that's because they can see prey better is uncertain, but you'll rarely find them in rips without pretty blue water on at least one side.

You'll learn that trolling through featureless blue water or water colder than 76 degrees is a waste of time. A rip with a good temperature break in depths between 120 and 400 feet is more apt to have bait. If no distinct edge appears on the most recent satellite picture, I'll check the wind direction and see if a prevailing easterly wind has pushed clear, warm water near some well-defined bottom structure along the continental shelf. Off the east coast of Florida, there is usually some bait on the rocky bottom structure of the shelf. If the water's blue and warm, that's at least a place to start.

Make sure you remember the most important part of rips isn't always the accompanying weeds. You'll have some of your best days on rips that are very difficult to follow, because there are no weeds showing you the way.

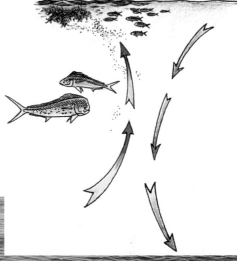

Look for rips with good current between 120 and 400 feet. They're the ones most likely to have bait in them.

Rips are formed at the boundary of opposing currents or otherwise differing bodies of water. They can be productive with or without weeds.

Flotsam and Boats

Flotsam can include anything from an abandoned raft to a coconut. Some types of flotsam are more likely to hold dolphin than others. Floating balloons rarely hold fish, but a slimy buoy, though smaller, is often encircled by green hornets. Before the age of environmental enlightenment, old-timers would put out mats of newspaper and drift along with them. We know better now, and search out boards, pallets and logs which are more productive anyway. The longer it's been in the water, the more likely it is to hold fish.

The best flotsam is usually the oldest, rich with attendant life.

A branch with attachments is a surefire dolphin magnet.

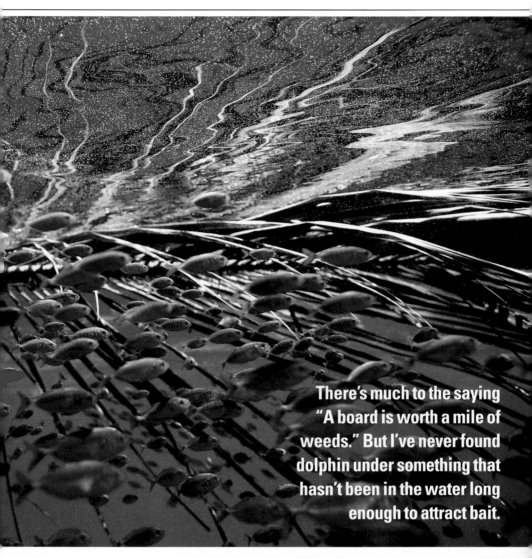

There's much to the saying "A board is worth a mile of weeds." But I've never found dolphin under something that hasn't been in the water long enough to attract bait.

A Flotsam Environment

Single pieces of flotsam are dolphin magnets on a barren ocean surface. Anglers search out floating objects like tree stumps forced into the ocean by tropical storms farther south. The longer a piece of debris floats in the ocean, the fishier it will be. Baitfish often attract to the "floater" first for protection, followed by species like tripletail and dolphin.

If you spot debris, troll lures by the flotsam to see if dolphin are hanging nearby. Then start chunking baits and dropping lures down below to see if dolphin are staging at deeper depths.

Once the boats congregate in an area, the fish may turn off. Finding your own hotspot is always better.

Fins up! Dolphin can raise their fins to discourage predators (left) or to help herd schools of bait (above).

Other Boats

There are many variables to consider, but the basic approach is simple: Find warm, clear water, then find surface structure—or at least bottom structure that holds forage fish—and pay attention to how hard the area you're in has already been fished. Remember to keep a detailed log. If you've had a good day, and found a good rip, take a look back at that day's satellite picture. Whatever you found, you'll want to know what it looked like on camera before your next trip.

Finding boats in a line either through radar or binoculars can help you pinpoint a productive rip. Remember that not only is etiquette important, but if you're fishing water that's already been fished, the hungry dolphin are already in somebody else's fish box. Nobody owns a rip. There's room to share, but you'll do better to fish a stretch that nobody's hit.

Finite areas, such as boards or isolated patches of weed, are another story. I've never seen a second boat be nearly as successful as the first. Finding your own spot is worth an extra few hours of running. SB

Keeping Your Distance

You can locate dolphin by following other boats. If you use this tactic, be considerate of others. Don't drag across another angler's trolling spread or cut anyone off. If a boat is drifting next to a floater, why not first hail the captain to avoid conflict? In this scenario, the fish have prob-ably already seen every lure and natural bait com-bination on the planet, anyhow. By getting in line and drifting live baits, you may catch your share. But keep in mind there are always other discoveries wait-ing to be made on the big blue.

CHAPTER 8

Selecting The Program

If you're trolling for schoolie dolphin, you need one set of rods, baits, tackle and teasers. If you're specifically after a big bull, you need another set. Selecting the program, figuring what to pull, when and on what, takes forethought.

Time is the primary limiting factor for a day offshore. You've got precious few hours, so you must learn to get effective baits in front of as many fish as possible. Make an honest assessment of your skill level and take it from there. Everything from weather to number of boats on the water should figure into your decisions. Let's look at the factors you'll want to consider before you select the program.

There's no better family fun on the ocean than encountering a batch of schoolie dolphin. Match the size tackle to the size fish and let 'er rip.

See DVD for more on choosing your attack.

Picking up your trolling speed and pulling bigger baits (right) can weed out the smaller fish.

Tactics

Nothing will fool as high of a percentage of dolphin as live-bait. If you're livebaiting you're probably not doing anything else. Kingfishermen have been highly successful fishing rigged ribbonfish along with live baits, but for the most part pelagic species are not as apt to hit a dead bait at two knots as the coastal-pelagic kingfish is. Trolling typically involves higher speeds. Running and gunning puts you on a high-speed hunt.

Fishing a bait from a rod in the T-top makes up for the lack of outriggers on many center consoles.

Every day has to be addressed individually. Do I know where the fish are? Are there too many boats on them? Are sea conditions going to restrict how well I can scan the surface or mess up my trolling spread?

Dolphin can be maddening as they attack anything that moves one day, while showing the snobbery of Martha Stewart the next. There are some generalities however that set dolphin apart from other selective fish.

Dolphin are hungry more often than not. More so than with other species, it will help you to devote more time to finding them and less time to slow-trolling expanses of ocean.

Live-baiting, natural-bait trolling, high-speed trolling, and running-and-gunning all have their place. The decision you have to make is: Are you going to be more successful covering a lot of water or presenting choice baits in a smaller piece of real estate?

This angler dragged
a heavy headed lure
at a brisk speed to
nail this gaffer.

Trolling

The problem with live-baiting is that you can't cover much water. Sometimes, you have to go exploring and that means trolling. You must adjust your trolling speed to the spread. Certain baits just run better at certain speeds; certain teasers work off different principles.

If you've decided to troll for bigger dolphin in a finite area, try building your spread around small-to-medium ballyhoo and maybe a single 8-inch mullet.

A natural mullet dredge, for example, is set up to pass pretty close inspection by a potential predator. A daisy chain of bowling pins is set up to trigger a response from a more aggressive predator. In the case of dolphin, bowling pins are supposed to represent a school of dolphin hot on the trail of an unseen victim. The pins really aren't set up to withstand close inspection.

If you're determined to find a big fish in a finite area, and you've got a crew capable of dropping back, build a spread around small- to medium-size ballyhoo and one 8-inch swimming mullet. Trolling speed will be somewhere around six knots, with teasers off both sides of the boat. While nothing is as alluring as a dredge, dolphin don't seem to be as picky as sailfish are. You'll notice a definite increase in the number of sailfish that rise to a natural dredge of mullet or ballyhoo, but dolphin seem just as fired

"Hey, somebody get up in that tower and find me a weedline to fish on."

Certain lures and baits pull better at certain speeds. A ballyhoo will never hold up at 12 knots. I've never been successful pulling a heavy high-speed lure at 6 knots. Generally speaking, the bigger a lure is, the less scrutiny it can stand up to. If you're giving the dolphin enough time to look your baits over, they better be rigged right.

Lures come in a wide spectrum of size, shape and color.

Circle hooks are rapidly gaining popularity.

Soft-plastic dredge teasers will attract dolphin.

up about a dredge of swimming shad tails as they are a bunch of high-dollar dredge mullet.

It's a good idea to pull a subsurface dredge behind a 48-ounce weight on one side and as many rubber squid on the other side as possible. Surface daisy chains are time-honored and very effective. Or you might take the time to rig a spreader bar with a couple-dozen small rubber squid, which also raise plenty of big fish.

Experienced captains spend more time trolling faster early in the season when the weather patterns are unstable. Rips can be hard to pinpoint when March winds are blowing. A cloudy sky obstructs satellite pictures, so it's time to put out some bigger baits and pick up the speed. The boats have also been at the dock, and nobody knows exactly where the fish are. You may run into a few

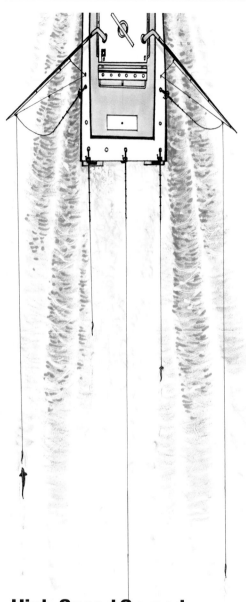

big fish in the "middle of nowhere," but it takes lots of nowhere to find the "middle." Pulling at faster speed means the small-to-medium ballyhoo and dredges have to be set aside.

Searching for only big fish or realizing you don't have the fish pinpointed changes what you pull. If I'm pulling in the 8-knot range, I choose bigger ballyhoo with dressing in front of them to keep them in the water. There's no mullet in the spread. At 8 knots or more it's usually impractical, if not impossible, to keep a dredge in the water. However, many anglers make the mistake of shelving the teaser idea. Rig 8 to12 ballyhoo or or soft-plastic shad tails

in a daisy chain with a weight in front of it. The commotion will draw fish in for a closer inspection. For dolphin, use more shad tails or plastic baits for teasers. You want the teasers to bring a big fish to the neighborhood, not set up a free lunch line.

Lures will rarely outfish a well-rigged ballyhoo, but sometimes lures are the way to go. Lures draw a more reactionary strike than bait. (Something's swimming away from me: I'd better grab it.) The same dolphin that crushes a lure at 12 knots probably wouldn't bite the lure at 5 knots. You need to pull lures fast enough that a big dolphin doesn't have time for analysis before it commits. Another consideration is that plenty of nice fish have bit ballyhoo left hanging in the outrigger while other fish were being fought. But they seldom strike a big lure just hanging in the water. For that reason, as well as the desire to cover as much territory as possible, don't go to an all-lure spread unless you've got miles of fishy water to cover and are prepared to troll at no less than 9 knots.

High-Speed Spread

Pulling two lines off your outriggers and three flatlines is a good high-speed spread. Stagger the baits to increase your presentation. Finding a blue hole, or clear part of your wake, will help you get more strikes.

When targeting a reaction strike, take your teasers out of the water. When a big bull chases down an imitation bait, you don't want him chomping down on a piece of hard plastic without a hook in it. Also, fish with tighter drags, stiffer rods and tighter outrigger settings. Unless weeds are a problem, you can replace the outrigger pins with No. 32 rubber bands. A No. 32 rubber band is strong enough to set the hook on a small-to-medium lure before it breaks. You'll probably only get one bite on a lure, so don't gamble with the slack that occurs when a pin releases. Something around the 8- to 12-inch size—like a rubber Mold Craft Wide Range Jr or a plastic C&H Stubby— are the perfect size to pull on 30-pound outfits and for a 40-pound bull. You'll also do well on the cedar plug, as well as artificial squid, but generally at a slightly slower speeds.

Remember to factor in how skillful your anglers are. Don't count on rookie anglers executing perfect dropbacks. If your anglers aren't skilled enough, let the boat set the hook by trolling fast plastics with fairly tight drags. If you need to outperform other boats working the same area, you need rigged ballyhoo and perhaps a few livies in the well. Be ready in case you come across a log or a short rip with a monster or two hanging on it.

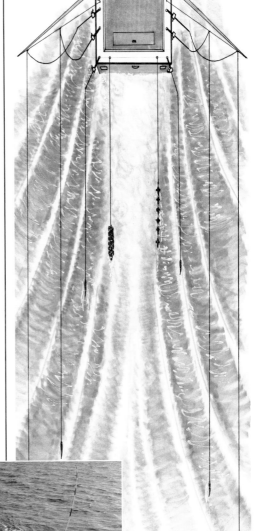

Natural Bait Spread

Try to run as many lines as possible off your outriggers when trolling naturals. When the release pin pops out, a short dropback happens automatically. Dredges and spreader-bar teasers work best at natural bait speeds.

Running and Gunning

You don't want to over-chum, just

Running and gunning involves running on plane until you find a promising board, weedline or rip. This is a great way for small-boat anglers to get the jump on larger vessels if seas allow. Once you find a promising spot or fish, start chumming. But make sure you have a

bait in the water as you chum. You want to hide hooks in cutbait or use the smallest hooks feasible in live baits. Also, use the lightest fluorocarbon leader you can get away with depending on the size of the fish.

Having live bait is important but not absolutely vital. Small "chummy" sized live sardines or threadfin herring—baits in the 4- to 6-inch range—are ideal. You want to carry a well full if possible. In lieu of live chum, cutbaits such as ladyfish, mullet, ballyhoo and sardines will work. This

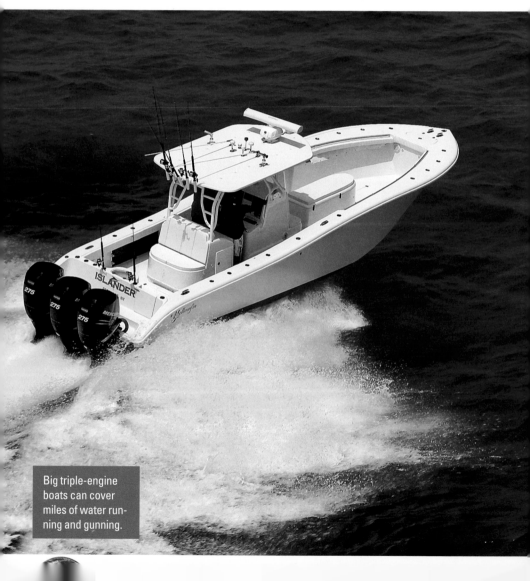

Big triple-engine boats can cover miles of water running and gunning.

dole out enough to keep them interested.

is a great way to get dolphin close enough to catch on fly and light spinning tackle. Jigs and streamer flies work well, as do swimming plugs.

You don't want to over-chum, just dole out enough to keep them interested. Unless the first fish is a monster, leave it in the water to keep the others around.

The best captains always seem to have luck on their side. It's one thing to troll up the most and biggest dolphin on the dock, but how in the world do the same lucky captains always seem to find the

"Golden Floater," the old barnacled pallet, or big tree holding enough nice dolphin to fill the box?

It's because the old statement about luck being when opportunity meets preparation has never been truer than in fishing. The best runners and gunners actually take a lot more into account before heading across the surface of the ocean with engines blazing.

First off, you need to understand that rarely is anything floating in the ocean by chance. Currents and wind work 24 hours a day at rearranging the

What to Do Once You Find 'em

How you handle what you run across will have a big impact on your day. Whether to approach a piece of structure and cast to it, or troll your baits past it, depends a lot on how much structure is in the area and what that structure is composed of.

On a busy Saturday, with other boats in the area, you're probably better off to put out a lure or two, and give each structure you find a "fly by" waiting to see if something comes out. You're also better off trolling if the area you want to fish is bigger than a cast or two can cover.

For an isolated floating object that you've found early in the day, and a chance at a single big fish, your first shot is going to be your best chance. Make sure you carefully approach the structure it's holding on. With a single piece of prime structure, say a lone weed patch, waterlogged pallet or tree, you're going to be better served by casting a jig, topwater lure or live bait. Always make sure you drop a jig or weighted bait down, even if you don't see any fish on the surface. SB

Check a floater or weed patch by trolling a single bait.

Make sure you keep a fresh bait ready to cast.

ocean's furniture. A good man with temperature charts will be able to figure out a place to start. Just think about how rarely you run into something floating in the ocean, truly in the middle of nowhere. Almost always the things you're looking for will be in the rip between two currents. Just because you can't see the rip, doesn't mean it hasn't pushed that log to just that spot. Study the temperature charts and start your search in the area with the most rips.

Secondly, running and gunning will only work on days with suitable visibility. If you're faced with a 3-foot chop, it may be perfect conditions to troll up a full fish box, but running and gunning is going to be darned near impossible. Remember, the higher you can get off the deck, the better you can see. Unless you've got a clear, uninterrupted view of the surface you'll be hard-pressed to pick up a log at any distance.

Remember if you're running into the prevailing wind and current, objects are coming to you at the same time you're running to them. Most rips off the east coast of Florida, for example, run from the southwest to the northeast. They generally track northwest in response to the usual spring/summer southeast sea breeze. Therefore, you'll usually cross more rips running southeast, as you head offshore.

Remember your chartplotter. You may think you're covering new water all the time, but I'll bet if you ignore your plotter for awhile, you'll end up covering the same water more often than you think.

Getting as far above the deck as possible with good binoculars and a great pair of sunglasses is vital for dolphin success.

When running and gunning, it's a good idea to stop every few miles and scan the horizon with good binoculars (above). Keeping fresh squid (left) chopped up for both bait and chum is a good idea. Just don't let it sit in the sun too long. It's always best for it to look and smell fresh. Remember it's easy to get too much of a good thing. Putting too much chum in the water can turn off the bite.

Keep That First Fish In the Water

School-size dolphin are apt to follow hooked fish to the boat.

Keeping a hooked dolphin in the water accomplishes a couple of things. First off when it's running and jumping, I don't think the other dolphin have any idea it's hooked. The dolphin looks a lot more like it's chasing something they don't see yet, but would love to eat.

Secondly it'll start spitting out whatever it's been eating, setting up an impromptu chum line, ringing the dinner bell for the rest of the school.

I certainly don't think they hang around saying goodbye to their old friend. It's all about trying to figure out what the hooked fish ate and how they can get it.

Regardless of the reason why, this fact remains. You'll increase the number of dolphin taken from a school by leaving a hooked fish in the water when casting more baits at the school. SB

Drifting

When you know exactly where the fish are, or recognize there are enough boats in the area to turn off the trolling bite, live bait is the number one choice. The same fish that watches cautiously as a couple of buddies fall to a trolled ballyhoo will fall for a frisky "livie" almost every time. Top live baits include goggle-eyes, blue runners, tinker mackerel, threadfin herring, sardines, mullet, menhaden and ballyhoo. If live bait is easy to catch, don't leave home without it. Just be aware that the time you spend catching bait or waiting for the bait boat is valuable.

The decision as to when to troll and when to drift usually comes down to time management. If you're looking for a relaxing Sunday afternoon listening to the ball game on the radio, drifting a couple livies with the motors shut off should be right up your alley. If you're trying to maximize your catch, then you've got to decide whether your time is better spent showing your baits to more fish or drifting some irresistible live baits in a smaller area.

Make no mistake about it, the more boats trolling an area, the less hungry the fish get. Anytime there's a regular procession of boats working a rip, you're smart to find the fishiest looking stretch and set up a controlled drift using your engines to keep you in position.

"Sexy" rips, logs or big sargassum mats scream for live bait. Slow-trolling live baits allows you to cover more water and excels along rips. It's best to keep three or four baits in the water at various distances and depths, usually under a kite or in a combination of outriggers, flatline clips and downriggers. Remember, trolling live baits is more like a controlled drift. It may require running on one engine and shifting to neutral often so you don't drown the baits. You can also drift fish, staying near productive looking structure. You may want to put a bait or two under a balloon or popping cork. Just be careful not to stay in one featureless spot. Waiting for the fish to come eat your livies can be a long day.

Slick calm with a little action up top? Send down a bait with a few ounces of lead and see what comes calling. It paid off for these anglers.

ddy falls for a ballyhoo, will often fall for a frisky live bait.

You can control where your bait goes and how deep by changing hook placement.
Just check to make sure the bait is swimming strongly.

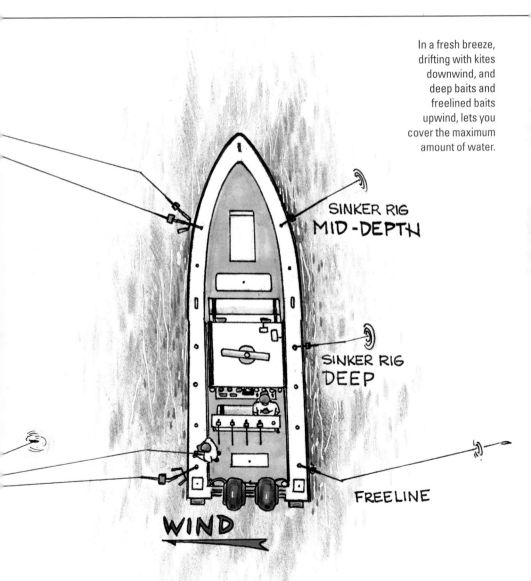

In a fresh breeze, drifting with kites downwind, and deep baits and freelined baits upwind, lets you cover the maximum amount of water.

SINKER RIG
MID-DEPTH

SINKER RIG
DEEP

FREELINE

WIND

CHAPTER 9

Natural Bait Rigging

There are three fundamental approaches to fishing for pelagic gamefish. You can fish live bait and stay in a well-defined area. You can put out high-speed lures and cover a hundred miles of water in a single day of trolling. In the middle of these two extremes is rigging and fishing natural baits.

The highest percentage of fish in any given area will fall for a kicking live bait. The smallest percentage of fish, particularly dolphin, will fall for a high-speed lure. Learning how to fish natural baits enables you to troll fast enough to show your baits to more fish, while still making a natural presentation to fool a high percentage of dolphin.

Rigging natural baits is a balancing act. What kind of bait is most appealing to the fish? How does each bait look at the speed necessary to make the rest of your spread look good? Does the tackle you're fishing match the size of the bait? Which rig gets you the best hookup ratio? These are all significant questions. Many anglers, myself included, will take a cooler full of well-rigged natural bait over any other method of attack.

Rigging natural baits is a balancing act. What kind of bait is most appealing to the fish? How does each bait look at the speed necessary to make the rest of your spread look good?

DOLPHIN

See DVD BONUS FEATURES for preparing natural bait rigs.

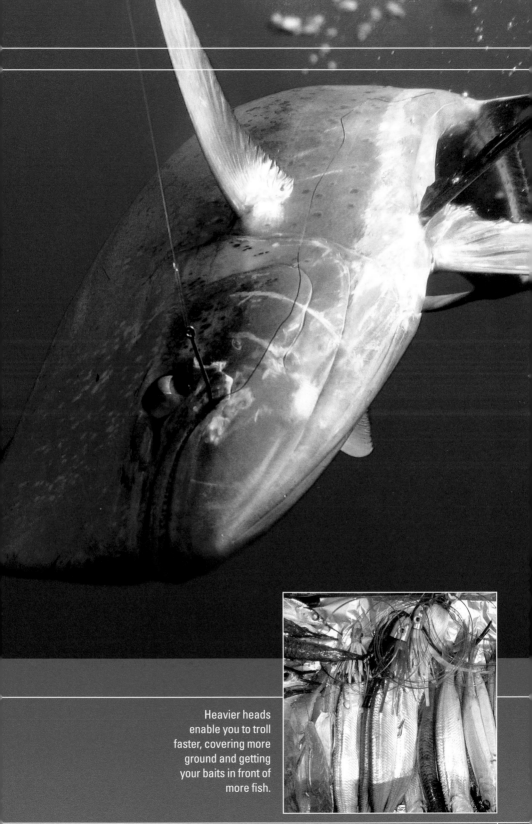

Heavier heads
enable you to troll
faster, covering more
ground and getting
your baits in front of
more fish.

Rigging for Success

Worldwide, an effective natural bait spread for dolphin is comprised of some combination of ballyhoo, mullet and belly strips from previous catches. Little tunny (a.k.a. bonito) are the most popular choice for strips because of their tough, shiny bellies. But mullet, dolphin and cobia bellies also work well.

Most anglers pull ballyhoo. Ballyhoo are a primary component of any pelagic fish's diet. They

Well preserved ballyhoo are great trolled baits, but never discount a fresh bonito belly strip.

are available just about anywhere there are fishermen. They are easy to rig, and they even come packaged according to size. "Dink" ballyhoo (usually around 6 inches) and medium-sized baits come in packs of a dozen. Selects, around 10 inches, come in packs of five. Horses, often a foot long, come in packs of two.

When you've got the option, always choose fresh ballyhoo. They're shinier, and you can pull them twice as long before they start to wash

out. If you're industrious, you can prep and even rig them before freezing some for future trips. If fresh ballyhoo aren't available, be picky when you buy frozen ones. Visit bait shops where you can pick your own packs from the freezer. Make sure the bags are vacuum-packed. Make sure the eyes are clear and the tips of the bills and tails are bright orange.

Dolphin don't have big mouths; a smaller bait will improve your hookup ratio. But there are many other factors to consider. A bigger ballyhoo is tougher than a small one; you can pull it longer and faster. Always consider your trolling speed when deciding what to pull. Remember, every time you increase your trolling speed 20 percent, without sacrificing the quality of your presentation, you should expect 20 percent more bites in a day's trolling. Bigger baits will also encourage bigger fish and discourage the peanuts. However, a 3-pound dolphin will attack marlin baits.

Unless you're also targeting wahoo at the same time, rig up with monofilament leaders. If you're also in wahoo water, keep a deep bait rigged with wire. Run the wahoo bait off a downrigger, behind a trolling weight. (Better yet, run a big-lipped diver.) Monofilament makes the baits swim better, gets more bites and results in a much better hookup ratio than wire leader. The next time you clean a dolphin and inspect its stomach cavity, notice that every big baitfish it swallowed went down their gullet headfirst. The fish will usually strike the bait from behind and then turn the bait around and eat it headfirst. That's much easier for the fish to do when the bait is rigged on mono, because of monofilament's suppleness. Sure, we lose some bites to kings and wahoo. But the box is fuller at the end of the day when we pull only mono leaders.

Avoid using trailer hooks or double-hooked baits. They don't swim as well and can spell disaster as a big bull thrashes around the cockpit, trying to bury a trailer hook in somebody's leg.

The experts agree. It's easiest to fool big bulls like this one with a well-rigged natural bait.

Prepping Ballyhoo

Prep ballyhoo slowly by defrosting them in chilled salt water. Never let your baits sit in fresh water.

When prepping your ballyhoo for rigging, give some thought to what your plan is for the day. First off, never wait until the day of the trip to rig baits. If the forecast looks good, rig at least four dozen baits the night before. Think about it. You just worked a zillion hours to get a day off. Then you invested untold dollars to get yourself in position for a great day's fishing. How could you not have enough baits rigged when the bite started? It's all about time management. And there's never time to rig baits once the bite is on. Never let a big fish swim into your spread without seeing something it wants to eat. It's like a football team driving 99 yards down the field and fumbling on the 1-yard line.

Prep the ballyhoo slowly by defrosting them in chilled salt water. Never let the baits sit in fresh water, as it will soften their flesh. The accepted method, for fear of trolling a stick or a spinning bait, is to separate the meat from the back along most of the spine. Plenty of dolphin are caught on baits that "swim like snakes." That said, I'm skeptical about the theory. Ballyhoo don't swim like snakes. I only push the meat away from the backbone from the anal fin back. I want his front half to stay rigid. Fish swim with their tails, not like a snake.

Be judicious about picking certain baits to brine. Yes, brining ballyhoo will make them last longer in the water. But you won't be very successful brining small ballyhoo. The tails get stiff and they won't swim. You will pull smaller ballyhoo a little slower, so settle for having them swim better and having to change them a little more often. The bigger baits—the ones you pull faster—seem to handle the brine better. Trolling faster than 6 knots with bigger ballyhoo, skirts and or dressings are heavier. Brining baits overnight in an icy cooler with a commercial brine helps them hold up better.

Eye Prep

Removing the eyes of a dead ballyhoo for trolling serves two purposes. Ballyhoo eyes, when left intact, have a tendency to bulge, causing the bait to spin. It's also easier to rig the copper wire through the open eye socket, rather than threading the wire around the eyeball. A handy device for removing the eyes and storing loose baits is an old hunting arrow. Push an arrow through the eyes of your ballyhoo to route out the socket and stack them down the arrow's length to store in your bait cooler. Remember to leave the nock or insert on the end of the arrow to prevent the inside of the shaft from filling with the discarded byproduct and its resulting aroma.

By storing baits in this manner, you're able to lay the baits in the cooler on their backs. Shake a layer of kosher salt on their stomachs to toughen them up for trolling. When you need a fresh bait to rig, simply pull one off the end of the arrow and rig it.

Bright, fresh baits are always an advantage and will stand up to the preparation routine. They also troll far better than frozen bait.

Ballyhoo Prep

By prepping baits you are trying to accomplish a few things. First, you're purging the stomach cavity of any waste and also popping out the inflated swim bladder.

Holding the bait in your hand facing belly up, gently squeeze from the front of the bait's stomach (1) and work from head to tail toward the vent. The stomach's contents will exit the bait through the vent (2).

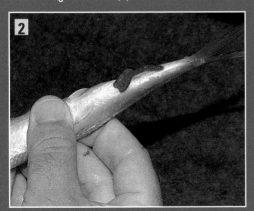

Next, turn the bait belly down in your hand and gently pinch the top of its back, working from head to tail (3). This action should loosen up the backbone. You will notice the depression down the top center on the fish's back pop up as you go.

Finally, rinse the bait off in salt water and flex it loosely in a snakelike motion (4) to complete. Before you attach this bait to a leader you should also remove the eyeballs to keep them from bulging out. This also provides an easy hole to pass your rigging wire through during the final rigging stage.

George LaBonte SB: Sailfish

Mono Ballyhoo Rig

Always begin with the highest-quality fresh bait, new leaders and sharp hooks. Small details make the difference at the moment of truth.

1 Insert your hook into the gill opening and exit the center of the belly with the hook point while pulling the eye of the hook into the body cavity.

2 Be sure the hook is lined up on the center line of the bait for straight tracking and that the throat latch isn't damaged.

Bring the copper wire out of the bait through the eye socket.

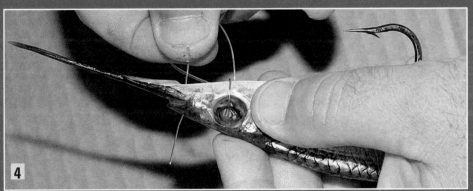

Make two wraps around the lower eye socket and gills to anchor the hook in bait. Push the wire up through the lower jaw and exit through the top jaw where it joins the head.

Make a couple of wraps down the beak and stop. Break the beak short and split the beak with your leader. Pull leader up into the split. Wrap the copper wire over the split and continue wrapping forward to the end.

Circle Hook **Ballyhoo** Weighted

As circle hooks become more popular for both live-baiting and trolling, many new tricks for rigging baits with them are being developed along the way. A popular technique for rigging ballyhoo for trolling involves preparing the baits without a leader attached. This method keeps your bait cooler more organized.

This approach is standard in Central America, where several dozen baits per day are required. It keeps the bait-box free of tangled leaders when the action gets hot. This rig is quick and easy and works like a champ for rigging a leaded "swimming bally-hoo." See the DVD for an alternative method using copper rigging wire; both rigs are extremely effective.

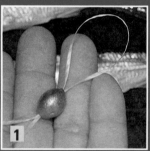

1 Double 2 feet of waxed rigging line and pass looped end through small egg sinker.

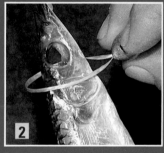

2 Pull the looped end over the bait's head and slip it under the gill plates on both sides of the bait.

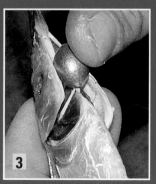

3 Slide the egg sinker down the rigged line so it fits between the gills forward of throat latch.

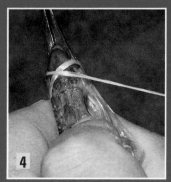

4 Bring the line's ends forward under the bait's lower jaw and wrap over top jaw. Keep line tight.

5

Pass both ends through eye sockets from opposite directions. Wrap gills over sinker and knot tight.

6

Tie another overhand knot in the two strands of line and pull it tight.

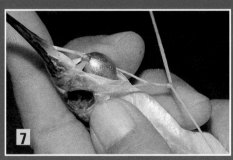

7

Pull the two ends away from each other; knot will slip down to egg sinker. Snug up and trim.

8

Break the beak off short and insert circle hook under x-shaped loop of thread on top of head.

Split Bill Ballyhoo

This extra step, added to a standard mono-rigged bait, will turn skipping surface baits into head-down swimmers. Being head-down gives it a swimming plug-like action without extra weight. Their simplicity to rig and lifelike action are tough to beat.

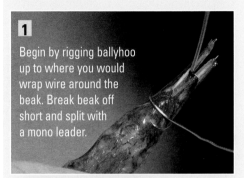

1

Begin by rigging ballyhoo up to where you would wrap wire around the beak. Break beak off short and split with a mono leader.

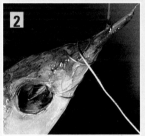

2

Continue wrapping the wire forward and lift the mono leader so you can wrap the wire in front of it.

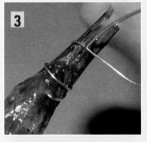

3

Make a single wrap in front of the leader and finish wrapping back toward the bait's mouth until you are out of wire.

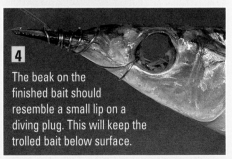

4

The beak on the finished bait should resemble a small lip on a diving plug. This will keep the trolled bait below surface.

Mullet

The two biggest dolphin I've caught both inhaled a split-tail mullet. An 8-inch mullet is almost irresistible to a 40-pound-plus fish that has already turned up its nose at your ballyhoo. The downside is, in some areas, it can be hard to consistently get good mullet in the spring when the bite is on. It's also more time-consuming to rig them.

Silver mullet make the best baits. It's a real trick to learn to debone them quickly; but rig them with a ½-once egg sinker and they'll swim so hard as to make your ballyhoo look anemic. The downside with mullet is that your hookup ratio is not very good. There's a lot more flesh for the hook to find its way through. You'll also have a hard time getting mullet to hold up at any trolling speed over about 6 knots. One owner of a bait-processing company told me that mullet will only hold up if

This big bull had no problem inhaling a deboned mullet.

they've spent most of their lives over sand bottom. He says mud in a mullet's digestive system makes the flesh soft. If you can get fresh 6- to 8-inch mullet, and you've got the time to rig them, they are highly recommended. There are also some very good commercially deboned and brined mullet, but they're pretty pricey.

BrineTime

Deboned mullet ready for salting in body cavity. This works much better with fresh mullet, of course.

Use coarse kosher salt liberally to cure mullet baits and strips alike. Salt will remove moisture from baits.

Flesh of jelly-like consistency will turn tough and durable, like partially cured beef jerky.

Prepping the Split-Tail Mullet

1 Cut a diamond-shape hole in top of bait. Cut inside from above the eyes back to the gills.

2 Make a cut between dorsal and anal fin as though you were filleting the bait.

3 Run the knife toward the tail, filleting only to the base of the tail.

4 Angle the blade downward and cut into the bone at the base of the tail.

5 Carefully slice back through the tail, separating into two equal laminates.

6 Insert knife up into body cavity and slice out backbone, ribs and excess meat and entrails.

7 Pull out this plug and a flat, hollow mullet remains. Rinse out and salt the inside.

8 Plug removed. Always freeze before rigging hooks, to allow bait to cure.

Rigging the Split-Tail Mullet

1

Begin by making a split in the bottom of the bait between the ventral fins to pass the hook through.

2

Pass the eye of the hook up through the opening and continue out through the wedge head opening.

3

Insert the leader end through hook eye, into the head and exit through the gills. Pass leader end through a...

4

...small $1/8$- to $1/4$-ounce egg sinker and place lead under chin of mullet. Tie loop knot or crimp to finish.

Egg sinker keeps rigged mullet bait from skipping too high, down where the dolphin can reach it.

Closing the Gap

To complete the rig, you'll need to tie the wedge closed. This step gives the bait a flat profile which makes it track straight and keeps it from washing out.

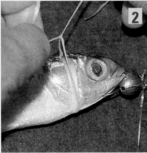

Tie the wedge cut closed by wrapping several turns around head with waxed rigging line and finish with tight overhand knots. Flatten head of bait on its side with palm of hand, before tightening rigging line.

Finished product is streamlined and ready to swim behind the boat.

Bait/Lure Combos

A n entire industry was born of fishermen's desire to make a ballyhoo look more natural to a fish. It may have started with lead-headed, feather-skirted lures which we used to keep ballyhoo in the water and holding together

What you want is something that makes your ballyhoo attract attention and help it hold together on the troll.

in a choppy ocean. Later came Sea Witches, Ilanders and untold numbers of other. They all work under certain circumstances, but again, it's a balancing act. What you want is something that makes your ballyhoo attract a fish's attention, hold together on the troll and not get in the way of a hookup. But in countless dives over tropical reefs, I've never seen a ballyhoo swimming around with a dressing on its head. Less can be more when it comes to dressing ballyhoo as naturally as possible,

especially when you catch a lot of fish on the dropback. When an angler takes the reel out of gear and drops the ballyhoo back into the fish's mouth, you don't want it biting down on a mouthful of lead and feathers. You also don't want the bait to sink unnaturally before it picks the bait up to swallow it headfirst.

If you're confident you know where the fish are, and how they're biting, rig some smaller baits on 100-pound mono. If you're pretty confident you won't have to search for miles between bites, smaller ballyhoo rigged on lighter leaders may get more bites and offer a better hookup ratio. If you're trolling slower over a school of fish, spending more time in the strike zone, you can pull more effective teasers. Your dropbacks also will be more natural than other boats pulling big baits, especially with heavy lures in front of their baits. Conversely, if the weather has kept the fleet home, and the sky has been too cloudy for a good satellite picture, use bigger baits that you can drag faster.

Ballyhoo combos are deadly on super slammers like this one.

Small Sea Witches and plastic skirts are the perfect match for small ballyhoo, while bigger baits swim better with heavier lures below.

Red Meat

Thirty years ago, stripping out the bonito from a day's catch was a task done with pride. Captains would stay an extra hour after every charter to strip out the bonito and salt them. This was partly because they couldn't always count on quality ballyhoo. But more importantly, we caught a ton of fish on them. The belly cavity of a bonito makes the best strips. The flesh is very tough and the skin is super shiny. Cut out the stomach cavity on each side and trim it down to a half inch. Cut a couple of willow-shaped 6- to 7-inch strips. Make sure you cut so when you troll, the wider end of the strip up at the front of the bait will move through the water in the same direction as the grain of the meat. Then, trim off another layer of meat so roughly a third of an inch thickness remains. Heavily salt the meat sides of the strips with kosher salt or commercial dry brine. Curing them overnight will make them great baits. Just put a layer of ice in your cooler, cover it with several pages of newspaper and set the strips skin-side down on the paper. Make sure the ice won't completely melt and leave your strips in fresh water.

Here's where the lures most people pull over the heads of their ballyhoo really shine. You need a skirt of some kind to keep the strip in the water and from curling up. Just make sure the skirt doesn't cover too much of the action of the strip. It's the wiggle that can drive a dolphin crazy.

Remember, you're trying to cover more water than the live-baiters, while fooling a better percentage of fish than the lure pullers. Learn to balance trolling speed, a natural presentation and baits that will give you a good hookup ratio. SB

Rigging Strip Baits

1 Start by making a minimal small hole in the front of the bait to pass your leader through.

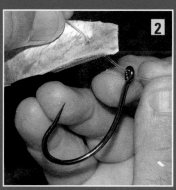

2 Pass your leader through the bait and your hook. A loop knot such as the perfection loop, below, is used to finish the rig. A crimp may also be used for heavier leaders.

Few baits can match the hookup ratio of a strip bait.

Prepping the Fillet for Strips

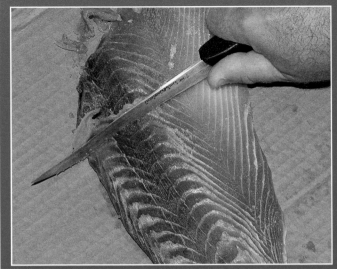

1 Start by cutting the bonito side down to ¼-inch thick. Next, scrape the fillet down to flatten and produce an even thickness. Always follow the grain of the meat.

2 Cut individual baits out of each side in the shape of a willow leaf. Baits can range in size from 4 to 8 inches. Plan your cuts carefully to get the most baits possible from each slab.

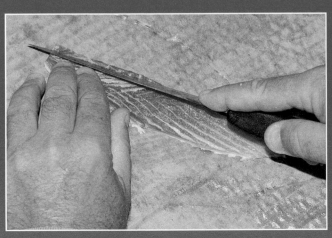

3 Fine-tune each bait to remove any ragged edges and bevel the edges of the meat, to improve action. Square off the forward point of the bait so it's pulled along with the grain.

CHAPTER 10

Teasers

Anything extra without hooks that you put out with your baits to attract fish qualifies as a teaser. A teaser is designed to either simulate baitfish or squid following your boat, or to make it look like a predator/prey chase scene is occurring, just screaming for the attention of any other predators in the area.

Dolphin have several personality traits that make them particularly susceptible to teasers. They are highly social, curious fish, and are always attracted to a good fight. They will invariably follow another hooked fish to the boat.

Dolphin can be attracted from long distances. Big dolphin will come greyhounding into the spread from more than 100 yards. Teasers help you draw more fish from farther away.

Dolphin have several personality traits that make them particularly susceptible to teasers. They are highly social, curious fish, and are always attracted to a good fight.

DOLPHIN

See DVD for more on dragging teasers.

Teasers can bring fish up by imitating schools of bait (above) or by creating surface commotion (below).

Bringing Them to You

I t seems like just about every topic we've covered concerning a good plan of attack has been about balance. Teasers are no different. Teasers that look great at 5 knots can't be pulled at 10 knots; conversely high-speed teasers are largely ineffective at slow speeds. In the last few years, teasers have changed from an afterthought daisy chain of 8 or 10 squids, to elaborate dredges, spreader bars, rubber dolphin and even painted boat fenders. For years, anglers in the northeast U.S. have caught everything from striped bass to giant tuna using dredges and spreader bars with hooks in the last bait. The method is finally catching on everywhere. It only makes sense that a big dolphin is more apt to see 20 baits going through the water than it is four.

Size Matters

Up to a point, fish are attracted to boats moving or drifting. Your boat is your biggest teaser. But too many boats in one area can make fish skitzy. The same fish that locks in on a boat from a couple hundred yards away is just as easily spooked off by 20 boats overhead all working a single weedline.

Boats that are trolling slowly (under 6 knots) are often better teasers than their captains realize. Because your boat is often your biggest attractor, you should pull at least one of your teasers close to the transom to catch the eye of anything checking out your bottom paint.

I run a 35-foot sportfisher. Often the owner's daughter will decide at lunch time that it's time for a swim. Invariably, if we've been trolling at natural-bait speeds, we find a small school of baitfish under the running gear when we jump in. Now that's a perfect teaser.

The slower you go, the more realistic your teasers have to be. A wary bull clearly spends more time inspecting baits trolled at 6 knots than it will when the baits are clipping along at 12 knots. Small dolphin have a tough time keeping up with baits pulled at 10 knots.

If you're trolling slowly, a bait school imitation dragged a little back from the boat is the best teaser. Baitfish generally swim in clusters, which is surely a big reason why dredges are so successful.

A big, noisy teaser, moving fast, will attract the most aggressive predators.

Baitfish generally swim in clusters, which is surely a big reason why dredges are so successful.

There's no such thing as a teaser too big to call in this slammer.

Deciding whether to pull a dredge or a daisy chain of bowling pins should be based on trolling speed.

The idea behind a dredge is to imitate a school of baitfish seeking the shelter of your boat. It gives predators a 3-dimensional view and has been the rage among dead-bait trollers for the last several years. Spreader bars loaded with rubber ballyhoo, squid or small skirts are great producers, but are pretty much limited to skipping across the surface.

This chain of Williamson rubber mullet is lifelike enough to be effective at different speeds.

Over the past few years, a tried and true northeast tuna secret has worked its way south. Using daisy chains or even spreader bars with a hook in the last bait can be a deadly way to rack up some dolphin in a hurry. Predators naturally pick off the last baitfish in a line. Southern anglers have finally tired of watching fish grab the last squid in their teaser chain. Some of the

This spreader is the perfect distance behind the boat. The bar is above the water and the squid are screaming for attention.

Squid Spreader Bar

Soft-plastic squid are extremely versatile. Pulled on 100-pound-test mono leader they make a good trolled bait, but they're even more effective when used on a teaser. Pulling a bar of squids imitates the same cluster of baits on the surface that dredges imitate below.

While fishermen in the U.S. northeast put a hook directly in the last bait on the bar, that can be a problem with a fish that jumps as much as a dolphin. I have been far more effective when we set a bait out in a position directly behind the bar. It never ceases to amaze me, that you can put 20 squid on a spreader bar and the last one in the line gets bit 90 percent of the time. The challenge is to keep your line from getting tangled in the bar while still having the bait appear as part of the school. You can have the world's best teasers, but it won't matter if the fish doesn't see the bait you want it to bite.

Pre-rigged spreader bars can sure make the mate's job easier.

Remember, the bigger presence you can make coming through the water, the better. A daisy chain of soda cans is better than no teaser at all.

more innovative have started trolling daisy chains, with hooks in the last bait. You can also use a daisy chain of rubber ballyhoo with a real ballyhoo trailing the fakes. It's a deadly tactic.

You can take the daisy-chain idea a step further by crimping 4 or 5 tiny Sea Witches or feathers along the length of a 6-foot leader with a medium to large ballyhoo at the end. A dolphin with a bad attitude likes nothing better than gobbling down a bait that looks like it's about to feed on something smaller.

Once you've started trolling too fast to pull dredges and spreader bars, you're limited to pulling straight-line teasers. This is where imitating a predator-prey relationship can really pay off. Once you speed up, you're better off imitating a predator following baits behind your boat. Draw

dolphin in with a daisy chain of dolphin-colored bowling pins, as well as a daisy chain of rubber dolphin. Pulling a small straight-running lure just alongside or just behind these teasers has put many a dolphin in the fish box.

Clear the Spread

Whereas it's best to leave your baits in the water when you have a fish on, it's going to be necessary to clear the area of teasers to prevent catastrophic tangles. Electric teaser reels may be considered an extravagance to some, but it's a huge help to be able to push a button and go help your angler while the teasers come in on their own.

For pulling dredges, it's hard to beat a downrigger. They've got the lifting power to pull against the tremendous resistance of a dredge, and the gear ratio to get them up quick.

For daisy chains or light spreader bars, a previously loved fishing reel clamped to an outrigger is sufficient. Remember to use one with plenty of torque. Even a spreader bar puts up a lot of resistance at 7 knots of trolling speed.

Remember, the bigger presence you can make coming through the water, the better. A daisy chain made out of soda cans is better than no daisy chain. The biggest factor in what you should pull for a teaser is the speed you're going to troll. The slower you're going, the closer your baits and teasers will be scrutinized. The faster you're going, the more fish you're likely to draw into the spread. **SB**

No teaser has called in more dolphin through the years than the squid daisy chain.

CHAPTER 11

Live Bait

O nce you've located dolphin, or at least narrowed your search area to a finite, manageable piece of water, nothing beats a live baitfish. There's little doubt a frisky livie will fool a higher percentage of the fish that see it than anything else you can put in the water. A 40-pound bull that has turned down every lure and every mono-rigged ballyhoo it has seen will lose its mind if it picks up the frantic vibration of a hooked live bait.

Just like most things that sound simple, there's a lot more to it than putting the hook in the back of a bait and throwing it overboard. Learn to do it better, and you'll be a better dolphin fisherman.

Just like most things that sound simple, there's a lot more to it than just putting the hook in the back of a baitfish and throwing it overboard.

See DVD for more on using live baits as pitch baits.

There's a fine line between having enough baits to fish with and overcrowding your livewell.

Types of Live Bait

L ive baits can be classified into two groups: those you can slow-troll and those that need to be drift-fished.

Baits you can slow-troll are best. Providing sportfishing boats with live baits for trolling has given rise to an entire industry of bait-catchers. These entrepreneurs truck fresh bait hundreds of miles. Lining up live baits before a tournament is essential for successful pros. For the most part,

these coveted high-dollar baits are either members of the scad family such as goggle-eyes (bigeye scad) or speedos (redtail scad). Various species of jacks are prized, most popular among these, the blue runner. Among other popular baits—which include sardines, cigar minnows, threadfin herring and menhaden—sardines are the strongest swimmers.

Don't be a snob when it comes to your live bait. Goggle-eyes may be worth $100 per dozen, but that doesn't mean a dolphin won't gobble down a lizardfish. In fact, I've seen a lot more filefish and bar jacks in the stomachs of dolphin than I have goggle-eyes.

Don't forget dolphin have been known to gobble down a mouthful of seaweed in order to eat the crustaceans inside. Jumbo live shrimp, eels

Goggle-eyes may cost $100 per dozen, but a hungry dolphin will als

If a dead ballyhoo makes a great bait, a live one can only be better.

and even crabs are in serious trouble if there's a hungry dolphin in the area.

Matching the hatch is great, but you'll never want to pass up a school of mullet hanging around the boat ramp. In northern climes, pogies on the beach are just what dolphin anglers want to hear. There's no easier bait to fill the well in a hurry than by castnetting a tightly balled school of pogies.

Some days you can procure bait right at the fishing grounds, catching small jacks and other fish along a weedline, for instance.

Wrecks, offshore drilling rigs and deepwater ledges also attract numerous species suitable for livebait deployment.

obble down a live lizardfish.

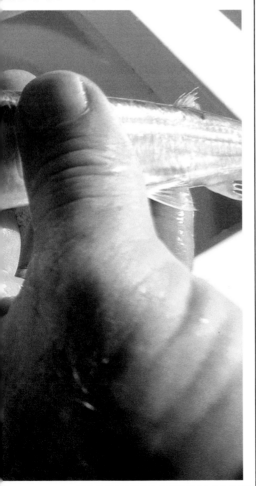

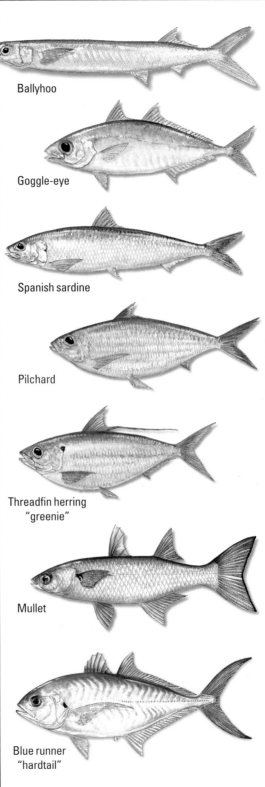

Ballyhoo

Goggle-eye

Spanish sardine

Pilchard

Threadfin herring
"greenie"

Mullet

Blue runner
"hardtail"

Catch Your Own Bait

North Carolina kingfishermen were among the first Americans to cast a chain of little gold hooks into a school of cigar minnows. (That may have been the place where anglers started using the Japanese sabiki rig in this country.) All the baits previously mentioned can

Try casting a sabiki or a tiny single jig around clumps of weed or other floating structure once out on the prowl.

be caught on various sizes and styles of sabikis. If you're intent on targeting the bigger scad, tinker mackerel or blue runners, you'll do better with the bigger sabikis, No. 14 through No. 16 for example.

Other species that take sabikis include cigar minnows (round scad), Spanish sardines, tiny jack crevalle and threadfin herring. These baits have accounted for a lion's share of big dolphin, especially off Florida. They can usually be jigged up by dropping smaller sabikis (No. 4 to No. 8) around offshore navigational markers, as well as shallow

wrecks and natural bottom structure. For most applications, a 2- to 3-ounce sinker on the bottom of the chain will get it near the bottom. But if you're fishing for baits schooled on the surface, you may want to try a ¾- to 1-ounce cigar-shaped weight.

While dropping your sabikis, you will also encounter various small bottom-dwelling species such as lizardfish, grunts and pinfish. Blennies and sand perch may also be in the mix. Dolphin eat every one of these species. But it's impossible to troll most of these baitfish. They will head straight back to the bottom. Therefore, they are best used for casting to a fish you've already spotted, or at the structure you're confident that dolphin are holding under.

If you find yourself struggling to catch bait, even after you've spotted baitfish rippling the surface or lighting up your bottom machine, don't hesitate to tip your sabikis with tiny pieces of fresh shrimp or squid tentacles. Even though the fancier sabikis claim to be made with real fish skin, sometimes a tiny tip of bait will load your rig even faster. Sardines, speedos, cigar minnows, blue runners and ballyhoo all respond well to ground chum. For ballyhoo, try a single hair hook (longshank No. 12 or so) with a tiny piece of squid behind the tiniest cork you can find.

Most bait species are associated with shallow water, but you can harvest bait offshore where you're fishing for dolphin. Dolphin hang around a floating pallet in a thousand feet of water due to the bait associated with it. Try casting a sabiki or a tiny single jig around clumps of weed or other floating structure.

Always try to have some live bait on board. If you don't have time to catch bait offshore, a piece of shrimp around the docks and cleaning tables in most marinas will produce enough pigfish, grunts and pinfish to have something to throw at a fish that refuses trolled bait. Having one crew member assigned to catching bait while everybody else loads the boat will often pay off in spades.

Pack a Bunch

It's difficult to reuse the smaller sabikis. They tangle something fierce and lose their shine after use. Make it a habit to carry enough sabikis to start the day with fresh ones, and to always have enough in case barracudas and kingfish pick off the hooked baits and take the rigs with them.

For catching a bunch of baits in a hurry, castnets are the way to go. But most anglers agree sabiki rigs deliver a friskier, longer-lasting bait (above).

Rigging Your Live Baits

Rigging a live bait can be as easy as sticking a hook through its back or as complicated as harnessing one under a kite. Hook selection has plenty to do with how well your bait will swim. Basically, the smaller the diameter of the hook shank and the lighter the weight, the longer the bait will last and the more naturally it will swim.

For most applications, a single offset-eye, live-bait hook is best. Most of your better hook makers offer a lightweight livebait hook which comes out of the box sharper than our grandfathers could have dreamed of. Choose the smallest diameter hook possible that will not straighten under drag settings. You want your bait to act as though it's a little impaired when a predator approaches, not struggling to stay upright with a hook big enough to shout out "something's wrong."

Take the time to learn to snell a hook. It keeps the pressure coming directly opposite the hook shank instead of off to one side because your knot gets off center. If you're going to hook a bait through the back or shoulder, select a hook with nearly the same size gap as the width of your bait. This helps prevent the hook from turning back into the bait, resulting in a missed bite. Due to increased danger to the fish and angler, avoid trailer hooks. If the crew is paying attention, they should be able to hook any fish worth catching on a single hook. For most live baits, an offset 4/0 to 6/0 livebait hook is deadly.

If you want to slow-troll near the surface, it's hard to beat a bait harnessed through the nostrils or eye sockets. Harnessing with waxed thread, dental floss or rubber band enables the bait to swim more unhindered, and helps it last considerably longer. It's just easier to swim with a thread through the nose

Whether or not to bridle a bait, or even where to hook it, depends mostly on how and where you want your bait to swim.

Ballyhoo (right) come with their own hook holders. Hooking a frisky livie through the nostrils (upper right) makes a great surface bait, while hooking a bait through the shoulders will send your bait deeper.

than a hook. Likewise for kite baits bridled through the shoulder. Many anglers believe a bridled kite bait with the terminal tackle completely out of the water is the ultimate presentation.

When you want your bait to swim down, hook it through the shoulder. Hooking it under the ventral fin will allow it to get deeper still. From a stationary boat, you can actually force your more active baits (sardines, blue runners) to swim toward the structure by hooking them behind the dorsal fin. When a bait gets off course, just pull it back gently to send it on a new course.

Slow-trolling livies can be an irresistible way to catch big dolphin, but you have to do it right. Actually, "trolling" live baits is a misnomer. What you're trying to do is less trolling and more controlling the direction in which your baits swim. Livebait pros know a live bait struggling to keep up with a boat is not natural. A flatline clip makes baits swim more naturally. It's perfect if baits are occasionally crossing to the other side of the boat or swimming up amidships. If your bigger baits (blue runners, bar jacks) keep swimming up to the transom, clip off the bottom half of the tail. That'll slow them down a little.

When fish are under the pressure of the weekend fleet, all fishing the same area, you'd better know where to buy or how to catch live bait. Nothing beats a fresh wiggler, so change live baits as often as your supply allows.

Troll the baits that normally travel fast (blue runners, cigars or sardines) and baby the ones (pinfish et al.) that aren't used to traveling. Always keep a hot one ready for when you spot that big blue-and-green forehead within casting range. It's as close to a sure thing as you'll find offshore.

Circle Hooks

Many anglers exclusively use circle hooks with live baits. You will almost never lose a fish with a circle hook unless you try to set the hook. Just reel down, and the hook should stick in the corner of the mouth. When using circle hooks, go up in hook size one or two numbers to ensure that the gap is wide enough. The only issue with circle hooks and dolphin with live bait is that smaller dolphin under five pounds have an issue getting hooked up. **SB**

Quickie Bridle

There's little debate among serious live-baiters that bridling a livie hooks more fish. The hookup ratio is higher, as the problem of the hook turning back into the bait at hookup is largely eliminated.

When slow-trolling a live bait, try running the smallest tie you can find through its eye sockets. It is a fast, easy rig setup and eliminates the need for a rigging needle.

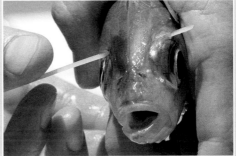

Pass wire tie (zip tie) through the top of the eye socket avoiding the eyeball.

Pull wire tie down snugly, but not tight enough to crush the eye socket and brain.

Insert hook under front side of tie facing up and trim the tag end of the tie.

CHAPTER 12

Artificial Lures

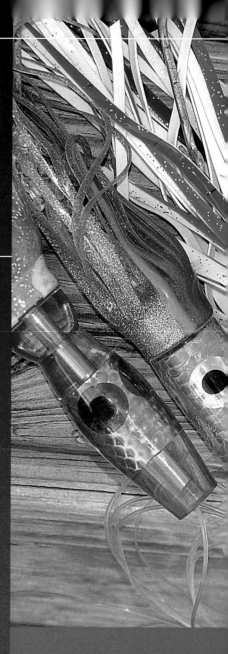

Artificial lures have evolved and improved tremendously over the last 40 years. When I started mating on charterboats, the only artificials we pulled were heavy feathers and a No. 3 Drone spoon, behind either a lead trolling weight or on a wire line.

Today, anglers can catch plenty of fish without ever learning how to rig ballyhoo. There are now incredibly lifelike artificials that imitate ballyhoo, mullet, squid and bonito—you name it. We still pull the wooden classics, but now there's a suite of high-speed resin and heavy metal-headed lures that can be trolled effectively up to 20 knots.

In between are other families of lures, some designed for casting, others for trolling deep, and still others for improving on natural bait rigs.

Today's anglers can catch plenty of dolphin without learning how to rig ballyhoo. There are now incredibly lifelike artificials that imitate ballyhoo, squid, mullet and bonito.

Having a lipped diver below your spread will not only get you strikes, but it will raise fish that may never have seen your other baits.

Soft Baits

Soft baits are as effective as they are fool-proof. They perform well with minimal terminal rigging and swim in a variety of trolling positions at a wide range of speeds. Body shapes, sizes and colors are available to represent many types of dolphin forage.

Some soft baits are fished alone, while others in combination with natural bait. Most of these are soft plastic. Fish will jump all over them on the dropback—that is if they don't gobble them completely on the first strike.

Dolphin will jump all over a soft plastic. They'll gladly gobble them on a dropback if they don't get hooked on the first strike.

The classic soft-plastic squid has been around for years. It's a great bait for tuna, sailfish and dolphin when running low on ballyhoo. Rig the 6-inch model on a 100-pound mono leader and pull it right behind your daisy chain. If a dolphin grabs it and misses the hook, drop it back. By the time the fish figures it out, you'll have him on. Green is a favorite color, but pink and flesh colors also work well. Today there are many companies making squid lures.

The Williamson 8-incher comes with a rigid hook lock, giving it a deadly hookup ratio. Adding a somewhat new dimension to trolling lures, Berkley offers a scented Gulp! squid in several sizes.

The Tony Accetta Jelly Belly has been racking up big dolphin for decades. It looks enough like a squid going through the water to fool a lot of dolphin. If you buy it unrigged, put enough beads or plastic spacers behind the lure so the hook rides right at the back of the skirt. Lots of pros rig the hook on a stiff leader, but the loose-hook rig seems to swim better and get more bites. You can troll the Jelly Belly with your natural baits or step it up to about 9½ knots. Try a shortshank 8/0 or 9/0 ultra-sharp hook.

Many lure-makers offer artificial ballyhoo, including some very realistic models pre-rigged on 130-pound

The classic big bait equals big fish scenario. This super slammer gobbled a Williamson soft-plastic bonito.

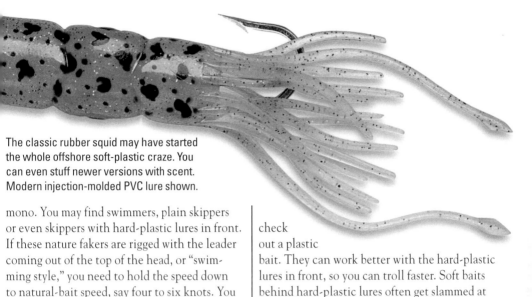

The classic rubber squid may have started the whole offshore soft-plastic craze. You can even stuff newer versions with scent. Modern injection-molded PVC lure shown.

mono. You may find swimmers, plain skippers or even skippers with hard-plastic lures in front. If these nature fakers are rigged with the leader coming out of the top of the head, or "swimming style," you need to hold the speed down to natural-bait speed, say four to six knots. You don't want to give dolphin too much time to check out a plastic bait. They can work better with the hard-plastic lures in front, so you can troll faster. Soft baits behind hard-plastic lures often get slammed at 10 knots.

Setting the Spread

BEST SPEED
6 to 8 knots

POSITION
Best fished up close behind teasers

LEADERS
Best fished on 100-pound mono

RUNNING MATES
Natural spread (mullet, ballyhoo, strips) and lipped divers

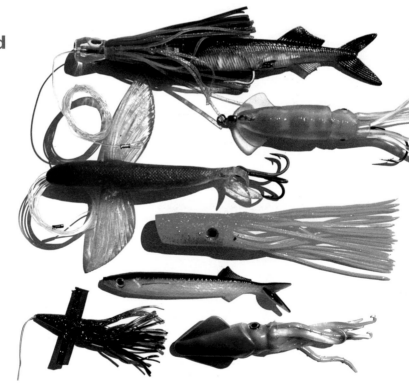

Just a few of the dozens of soft plastics available for trolling. With a spread out of these you can carry your baits in your suitcase.

Headers

Headers, as the name implies, are lures whose primary job is to fit over the head of a ballyhoo, strip or mullet. They are made of everything from chicken feathers to mylar. It's generally the weight and the shape of their head that determine when they're most effective.

The first header I'll usually reach for is a $^1/_8$- to ½-ounce Sea Witch. A Sea Witch is nothing but nylon hair tied to a small, slightly elongated egg sinker. Several lure makers sell these under different names, and some captains swear by their own hand-tied creations. The beauty of a Sea Witch is

that it covers the head of the ballyhoo, helping to keep it from washing out. When you drop it back, its light weight keeps the bait from sinking too fast. It fills out and flutters in the water, making a bigger target for a second strike. Many colors are available to suit your needs, but blue-and-white always seems to be effective.

The next group of headers comprises those which change the profile of the bait and the way it swims. In this group, the most effective lures I've

The weight and shape of their heads are what makes headers effective.

Softer heads mean dolphin will hold on to them a second longer on the dropback.

Setting the Spread

BEST SPEED
5 to 9 knots

POSITION
Both long and short outriggers

LEADERS
Best fished on 100-pound mono

RUNNING MATES
Naked baits, soft plastics and lipped divers

Different shaped heads for different speeds. All are light weight to keep them from sinking on a dropback.

found have flat or concave heads and are generally made of rubber or plastic. The C&H Lil' Stubby and Lil' Bubbler and Mold Craft and Boone small rubber chuggers are my favorites on smaller baits, with a C&H Alien getting the nod for bigger baits. (The latter is a 12-inch lure. With any of these, trim the skirt so it ends just past the bait's gills—you're trying to dress your bait, not cover it up.) The beauty of these lures is they create a bigger profile in the water. When pulled at the right speed, they create a bubble trail you and the fish can see from a distance. Once again the light weight and softness of these baits make them easier for a fish to find. I'm certain they'll hold on to a soft rubber chugger a split second longer. Furthermore, you can troll headers faster than naked baits. At 7½ knots, you'll cover 30 percent more water than you will at 5 ½- to 6-knot naked-bait speed.

Heads Up On Headers

Make sure the size of your header matches the size of your ballyhoo. Remember you're dressing up your ballyhoo, not covering it.

When it comes to choosing the right header to slide over the head of your bait, remember the old saying about too much of a good thing. Headers are actually as much about trolling speed as they are about attracting dolphin. A dolphin has to be able to pick up a baitfish swimming through the water without window dressing. Its very survival depends on it.

Certainly the bubble trail left by a concave-headed lure in front of your ballyhoo means your bait can easily be spotted. The extra trolling speed you can add on, once you've got your baits covered to prevent wash out, is just as important.

Feathers

Feathers are timeless lures still available today in a stunning array of sizes and configurations. I've fished $1/8$-ounce sizes as headers or on their own for small bonito or tuna, and large 16-ounce feathers as a high-speed wahoo lure.

This is hardly a new class of lure. Pacific islanders have trolled feathers for centuries. But, many contemporary experts say there's still nothing better than a natural feather skirt. Chicken, turkey, and goose feathers from Zuker, C&H, No-Alibi and others are as deadly as ever.

A string of six $1/8$-ounce feathers spaced on the leader, about a foot apart, with a 4/0 shortshank hook in the last one is great on both schoolie dolphin and tuna. A $1/8$- to $1/4$-ounce black feather over the head of a fresh bonito strip will allow it to flutter on the surface at 6 knots, driving dolphin crazy and giving you an excellent hookup percentage.

One- to 3-ounce feathers will allow you to pull a medium ballyhoo faster, and they won't sink too fast on a dropback.

Once you get heavier than 3 ounces, you're probably better off pulling feathers by themselves. The 4- to 6-ounce models make great run-and-gun lures, and the jumbos (8 to 12 ounces) are a weapon at higher speeds.

My personal favorite? Nothing I pull seems to consistently outfish an 8-ounce black-and-orange No-Alibi. Fish it with a standard 9/0 hook, on a wire leader for less water resistance, keeping the lure in the water better. All-white seems to be another great choice.

The No-Alibi Dolphin Delight is a South Florida staple. It's really a flat-head feather with a squid skirt over it. But it's shaped to ride flat and slide across the surface. Make no mistake about it, dolphin love a bait skittering on top, and the Dolphin Delight has been many a dolphin's last supper. It comes in many colors, but my favorite has always been green-and-gold. The Dolphin Delight comes in $1/4$-, $1/2$- and $1 1/2$-ounce models. Troll at speeds that keep it gliding on top but not jumping out of the water. It can also be rigged ahead of a ballyhoo, either real or plastic. For this lure, try an 80-pound mono leader ahead of a 7/0 standard ring-eye hook.

Make no mistake about it, dolphin love a feather bait skittering on the surface.

Heavy feathers shine brighter the faster you pull them. Their lifelike movement through the water has never been duplicated.

Setting the Spread

BEST SPEED
5 to 8 knots for "header feathers," 9 to 12 knots for heavy "stand alone" feathers

POSITION
Shotgun and farther, up to 200 yards

LEADER
Singlestrand wire helps keep the feather in the water

RUNNING MATES
Heavy metal head, concave-face medium-size lures, lipless swimming plugs

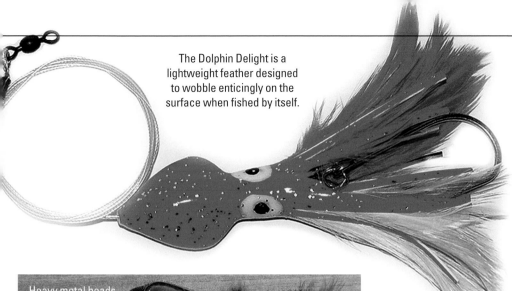

The Dolphin Delight is a lightweight feather designed to wobble enticingly on the surface when fished by itself.

Heavy metal heads are better pulled alone, while lightweight feathers can make a dead bait look alive.

FeatherTalk

There are many factors that help decide what type of feather to pull.

I've had excellent success pulling the smallest $1/16$-ounce feathers in a daisy chain with a ballyhoo "chasing them" through the water. Somewhat larger feathers are excellent over the head of ballyhoo, and the biggest are best pulled alone. Why are these lures so effective?

Certainly their weight helps hold the bait down in the water, and their color is a factor, but I've often had my best success on a feather once it's been chewed to oblivion. My advice? If they keep hitting it, you keep pulling it!

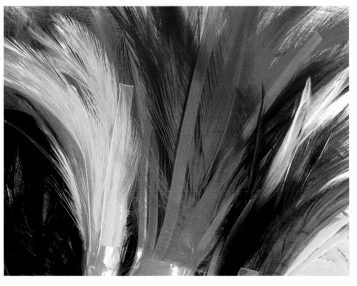

High-Speed Lures

will run because of line diameter's displacement. When dealing with speeds faster than 11 knots, it's often necessary to use heavy metal-headed lures and singlestrand wire leader to keep the baits in the water.

One standard is a Mold Craft Wide Range. The best size for dolphin is the 9½-inch model, but never fail to take seriously the big bait equals big fish theory. There have been some beautiful dolphin caught on the 12½-inch Senior model. The beauty of this bait is that it catches fish from 4 to 14 knots. At 9 to 14 knots, it really excels. It's a straight runner, and like most plastics it's most effective if it's just breaking the surface often enough to create a bubble trail behind it. Many anglers believe the hookup ratio is better on this bait than most artificials, as the soft-plastic head may encourage fish to hold on to it long enough to get the hook. Dolphin may be very cannibalistic, because top color patterns include green-and-yellow and green-and-black.

A big bull does a little sky-scraping after he slams a high-speed lure.

There are plenty of advantages to trolling high-speed lures. You can cover more water and potentially show your baits to more fish. You can run to that circling frigatebird without picking up your baits.

The strike you get on a high-speed lure is usually an "all-or-nothing" strike. When a dolphin slams a lure at 12 knots and the reel starts screaming, you'll understand why high-speed lures are gaining popularity.

You don't need more than 50-pound tackle or 200-pound monofilament leaders. As a general rule of thumb, lure action is better on lighter leader. The heavier the leader, the higher in the water the lure

The C&H Alien is also on our experts' lists, and again its beauty is in its versatility. Like the Mold Craft, it's a very lightweight straight runner, which means you can pull it a little slower and still keep it near the surface. Green-and-yellow is the hot color, and you can keep the 10½-incher in the water at higher speeds. Stick with the singlehook stiff rig and pull it at 8 to 11 knots.

The Pakula Mouse is a little different. Its resin head is heavier than either the Alien or the Wide Range, which means a little faster trolling speed is necessary. It also has a slanted head, which gives it a side-to-side wobble. The 12-inch

A heavy metal head has fooled
many a good dolphin at 12 knots.

You can't pull a lure big enough to discourage a medium-size dolphin if it's hungry.

Setting the Spread

BEST SPEED
9 to 13 knots

POSITION
Both flatline and short riggers

LEADER
Best pulled on 150- to 200-pound mono (100 pound for smaller lures)

RUNNING MATES
Heavy feathers and lipless swimming plugs

brown-black-orange color pattern is a favorite. Keep your speed up between 9 and 12 knots.

If the ocean's choppy, or you need to cover ground in a hurry, the heavier metal heads like the Boone Hoo Lili or a good old 6-ounce leadhead feather will keep you in the game. Often, a plain red-and-black 6-ounce feather will out-perform lures that cost more than your first pickup truck. If you're moving faster, remember to run your feathers rigged with a wire leader. The thin-diameter wire cuts through the water and keeps the lure from bouncing out of the water.

A Case for Single Hooks

Plenty of fishermen will argue with me, but I pull single hooks in all my lures, usually on a stiff rig. The second hook of a double rig will cost you as many fish as it catches, by one hook pulling out the other as the battle wears on. In terms of hook selection, an ultra-sharp, thin-diameter hook penetrates most easily. However, thicker diameter, bigger hooks withstand the shock of a strike at high speeds. A single 10/0 to 12/0 stainless steel 4X hook does a better job of keeping a big fish hooked.

Single hooks are also much safer and easier for the mate to remove. Aboard the *Dos Amigos*, we have a self-imposed limit of two dolphin per person. If we have our limit and have another hooked fish alongside, I sure don't want somebody trying to get two hooks out of a hot fish that we're trying to release.

Casting Lures

Lures are less about what to throw, and more about where to throw it.

Hungry dolphin, which means most dolphin, will strike most lures you put in front of them. The pattern and action aren't as important as the hooks and casting distance.

If I'm going to throw a lure at a log that's holding dolphin, my favorite would be a walk-the-dog type, such as a Rapala Skitterwalk. Action isn't critical, so I'll remove the front hooks altogether and replace the back treble with a 5/0 livebait hook.

Chuggers, too, are terrific dolphin lures. There are saltwater varieties equipped with substantial hooks, but even inshore models will perform, assuming you upgrade the hooks.

If the dolphin have been pressured, or just don't want to bite, it's jig time.

If there's a better jig than a Storm Live Mackerel, I've never seen it. It has an extremely realistic mackerel pattern and a soft-plastic body molded over a weighted hook. I don't, however, believe the action is as important as being able to cast a good distance. A standard jighead with any swimming-type rubber tail will get the job done 90 percent of the time. And it seems this class of lure grows by the year, with new manufacturers bringing out more realistic selections every day.

The classic bucktail is a time-proven dolphin-slayer—inexpensive, durable and versatile. For tight-lipped fish, it's a cinch adding a strip of natural bait to the bucktail.

Lit-up schoolies mean this soft plastic is about to be consumed.

Throw a Soft Bait and See What Happens

Soft-plastic lures are showing up more often in dolphin fishermen's arsenals over the last few years and more boats are not even carrying bait.

Throwing a soft plastic, either scented or unscented, into a school of dolphin will almost always get an immediate strike. After a few fish have fallen for the same lure, it may be necessary to change style or color. As a last resort, adding a strip of natural bait will fire the school back up.

Try to pick out a lure that has enough weight to cast, but not so heavy it sinks too fast, causing the school to follow it down. The whole beauty of throwing soft plastics at dolphin is seeing the changes in their behavior before they attack. It's bluewater sight fishing at its best and fun for the whole family.

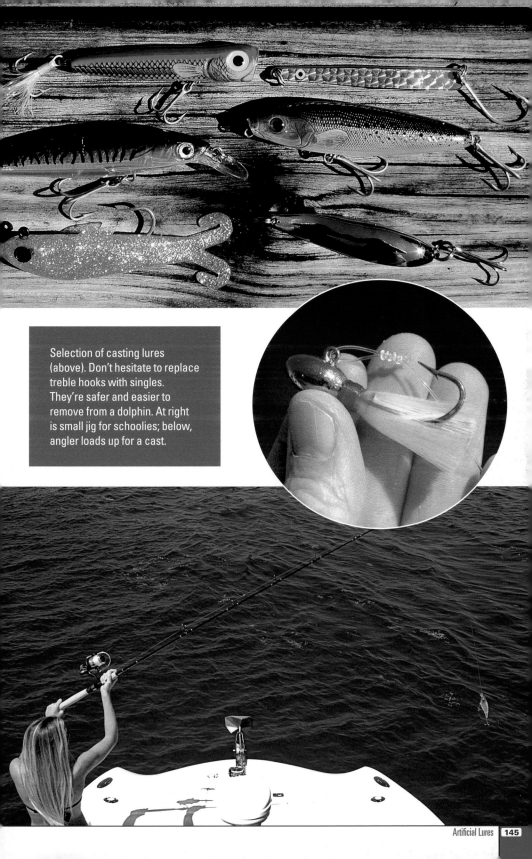

Selection of casting lures (above). Don't hesitate to replace treble hooks with singles. They're safer and easier to remove from a dolphin. At right is small jig for schoolies; below, angler loads up for a cast.

Swimming Plugs

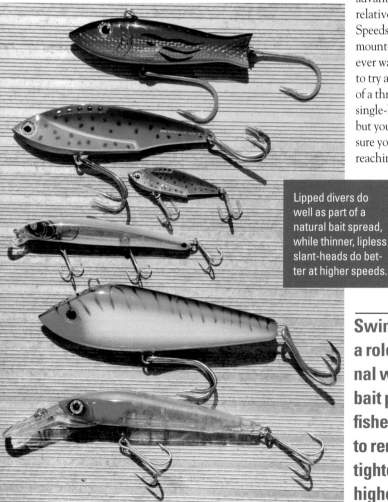

Swimming plugs have a role in your arsenal whether you're a bait fisherman or a lure puller. The trick to remember is, the tighter the wobble, the faster the speed.

I don't like downriggers for dolphin, and I'm not nuts about trolling weights or planers. The biggest dolphin we ever hooked on *Dos Amigos* was actually hooked on a planer, but once the bull started jumping with the planer flying through the air, a disastrous ending wasn't far behind. A metal-lipped magnum Rapala dives as deep as most downriggers run; deeper-running big dolphin jump all over them. I've also done well with Yo-Zuri's Hydro Mag. Whereas the Rapalas do best at 6 knots, I've pulled the Yo-Zuris up to 9 knots.

Once you speed up past 8 knots, the Cairns Swimmer type is great on big dolphin. One advantage of the Cairns (or close relatives Yo-Zuri Bonita and Braid Speedster) is the single hook that's mounted on a swivel. You don't ever want to reach in your fish box to try and take a six-hook lure out of a thrashing dolphin. Using the single-hook swimmer style is safer, but you're still better off making sure your fish is expired before reaching for the hook. The new long-handled hook removers reduce the hazard somewhat.

Colors? It's your pick. I like mackerel and hot pink (especially pink in the Mann's Stretch 25). **SB**

> Lipped divers do well as part of a natural bait spread, while thinner, lipless slant-heads do better at higher speeds.

Swimming plugs have a role in your arsenal whether you're a bait puller or a lure fisherman. The trick to remember is, the tighter the wobble, the higher the speed.

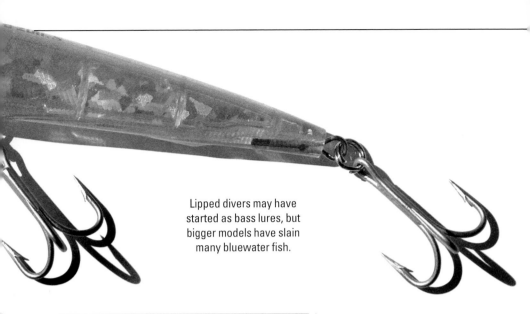

Lipped divers may have started as bass lures, but bigger models have slain many bluewater fish.

Set the Depth

There are a few different ways to change the depth a swimming plug will run . Metal lipped divers such as the Magnum Rapalas can be forced deeper by bending the lip down. When buying plastic-lipped divers remember the bigger the lip, the deeper the dive. For blade-type lures with several holes to choose from when attaching your leader, the trick is to place the leader farther back, the deeper you want it to run. Remember, all swimming plugs wobble with more action and dive deeper when fished on a wire leader with braided line and a stiffer rod.

Setting the Spread

BEST SPEED
6 to 8 knots for lipped divers; 8 to 11 knots for lipless swimmers

POSITION
Poor outrigger bait. Run tight to transom or way back off rodtip

LEADER
Singlestrand wire gives swimming plugs more wobble

RUNNING MATES
Natural baits with headers and soft plastics for lipped divers. Feathers and high-speed lures for lipless divers

CHAPTER 13

The Perfect Flyrod Target

What could be better on a fly rod than a gorgeous, delicious fish you can sight cast to? A fish that will hang around the boat long enough so you can gauge the weight of the fly rod needed, before you cast? A fish you can count on for screaming runs and all the jumps you can handle?

Too many fishermen make the mistake of trolling baits past a piece of surface structure, in an attempt to determine if there are dolphin present, hoping they can then cast a fly at it. There may only be one or two fish around. Even if there are plenty of fish present, the biggest and most aggressive of the school will almost always feed first. If you're determined to catch a big dolphin on fly, keep your rod and fly in hand, and be ready to cast at a moment's notice.

> If you're determined to catch a big dolphin on fly, keep your rod and fly in hand, and be ready to cast at a moment's notice.

Here's a bull taken from a pair of fish that came in hot and heavy on a trolled teaser.

Flying for Dolphin

When the fish piles on the fly, wait until you feel its weight and then strip strike.

Match your flyfishing techniques to the way dolphin feed. If you don't have the fish in sight, trolling with teasers or hookless baits is the best way to get them in flycasting range. Keep the boat in gear, and keep a couple dredges, daisy chains or hooked baits in the water with your eyes glued to them.

Before a dolphin shows up, strip off enough line to send a fly just past the teaser. If your deck isn't completely clear, I'd recommend a stripping basket, Line Tamer or at least a 5-gallon bucket, sans handle. As soon as a fish shows up, the mate should bring the teaser closer to the boat while you get ready to fire a "snap cast." To perform a snap cast, strip off 1½ rod lengths of fly line and hold the fly between the thumb and index finger of your free hand. Hold the line against the rod so the pressure of your back cast pulls the fly from your fingers and the rod loads so the forward cast can be made. Strip the fly in 6-inch increments in front of the dolphin. When the fish piles on the fly, wait until you feel its weight and then strip strike. If you lift the rod, you may pull the fly away and you can't get nearly as solid a hookset.

Two fly fishers battle schoolie fish that were kept alongside by chumming. Below, poppers can turn dolphin on.

Dead Boat Casting

A piece of floating structure sets up an ideal scenario for fly fishing for dolphin. Reel in the conventional lines; if you've got outriggers stand them up. This is where center-console boats really shine. Communication between captain and angler is mandatory. Move your caster to the bow. Motor your boat slightly upwind keeping the breeze so that it's not blowing into the casting arm. In case the dolphin aren't committing to the fly, it's a good idea to have a big, hookless plug ready to tease the fish with. A fish that won't leave his board to chase a fly will sometimes charge into open water after

Quality large-arbor reels with smooth drags are a must for fast pickup during a dolphin fight.

> **Either a floating or intermediate sinking line works for fish at the surface. For deeper fish, "dredge 'em up" with full sinking lines.**

something loud and splashy. A lit-up, aggressive fish is much easier to entice with a fly. Of course, a big popper can make a ruckus, but can be a pain to cast or work quickly enough. Either a floating or intermediate-sink line works for fish on the surface. But often dolphin hold far below the structure. You can "dredge up" interest by sending a Clouser Minnow way down and working the fly vertically through the water column. Live chumming around mats of sargassum or other structure is a surefire way to attract fish into range.

Rigging Up

Different-size dolphin are a lot more fun if you have the fly rods to match their size. For schoolies, a 6- to 8-weight rod can be a hoot. Usually, you need a floating fly line with about 8 feet of leader tapering to 12-pound-test and a 10-inch piece of 30-pound mono or fluorocarbon to prevent chafing. For dolphin 10 to 20 pounds, you'll want to upgrade to at least a 9-weight rod. Ten- to 12-weight rods are really best for fish over 10 pounds. Use 16-pound leader and a 40-pound shock leader. Make sure to have at least 200 yards of Dacron or polyethylene line for backing, which a big fish will make disappear fast.

If you're after a true giant, you may want to employ a 12-weight rod and a matching reel with a large disc drag system. Deciding between an anti reverse or direct drive is a matter of personal preference. You'll want to attach a short piece of 80-pound mono to the end of your leader, as the fight with a big bull can go on for quite a long time. **SB**

Angler palms the spool as a bull takes off. This large arbor reel ensures even drag pressure as backing melts away.

Down she (or he) goes! A big dolphin will sound, so choose a rod of adequate size with good power in the butt.

Flies **for Thought**

Small epoxy minnows will generally work on schoolies and a single 2/0 hook suffices. For bigger dolphin, a big Deceiver, Clouser pattern or large popper will work well. A word of caution on the big poppers though, they offer so much wind resistance they can be difficult to cast. It's much easier to set the hook with a streamer. Make sure to use a loop knot on all streamers to ensure maximum fly action.

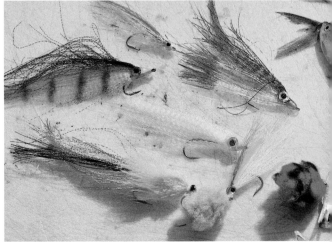

An array of baitfish streamers will work, but sometimes a particular size choice makes all the difference to the fish.

CHAPTER 14

Hooking, Fighting And Landing Fish

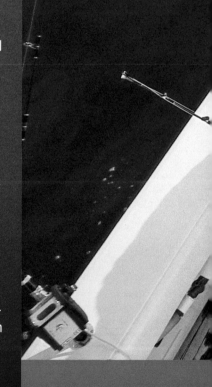

You've worked all week for this. You've saved every spare penny for who knows how long. You've bought the drinks, rigged the baits, and gassed up the boat. You've stared at your baits until you started dozing off in the sunshine. Suddenly a big blue-green head starts charging across the wake after your outrigger bait. Here comes your chance. Here comes the reason why we do what we do.

Hooking, fighting and gaffing amount to the end game when it comes to dolphin fishing. They bite differently than most fish, they certainly fight harder than most, and they may well be the most dangerous fish you'll ever encounter on the end of a gaff.

Once you've decided you want to catch more than one dolphin at a time, you'll need to learn how to fight multiple fish, while keeping the rest of your lines in the water. It's one of the hundred little things that make the difference between weekenders and the guys who fill the rack at the marina with big dolphin.

It's one of the hundred little things that make the difference between the weekenders and the guys that fill the rack at the marina with big dolphin.

DOLPHIN   See DVD for more on hooking, fighting and landing dolphin.

Pretty water, pretty girls, and pretty dolphin. Some days everything just goes right.

Here He Comes!

Of the many things I love about dolphin, the fact you often see them charging a bait from a hundred yards away ranks near the top. Whether it's a dolphin or a billfish, you've got a huge advantage anytime you see a fish come into

Just what a mate lives for. A big dolphin broadside to the boat awaits a clean gaff shot.

your trolling spread. When I see a dolphin come greyhounding after an outrigger bait, you can get the grease hot back home. We're gonna be eating mahi tonight.

I learned how to troll ballyhoo long before we'd ever figured out livebait fishing or bluewater lure fishing. Our boats wouldn't go slow enough to troll livies; we'd never heard the word sabiki. The measure of a good mate back then largely depended on his ability to execute a successful dropback. If you could see a fish coming, be on the rod as the line popped out of the outrigger clip, and feed it to him, you could almost always find a charterboat to work on.

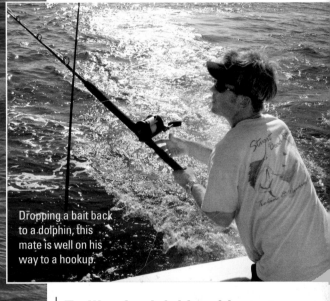

Dropping a bait back to a dolphin, this mate is well on his way to a hookup.

Trolling for dolphin with most lures is pretty much a "drag-'em-and-snag-'em" method.

As the years have gone by, I've come across fewer young mates who know how to perform a successful dropback. Keep in mind, trolling for dolphin with most lures is pretty much a "drag-'em-and-snag-'em" method. The hooks are usually set near the back of the lure. Once a dolphin grabs it, the 'phin is usually as hooked as it's going to get. Even if a dolphin misses the hook when striking a lure, one of two things will happen. Either the bull or cow will try again or it will give up after biting into something unnatural. Trolling lures for dolphin may be the ultimate laid-back trolling. When the rod bends over, your fish is hooked.

Eyes on the weedline, ears on the cell phone or VHF, the captain zeros in on the action.

For the ballyhoo fishermen, things are a little more complicated. The hook in a well-rigged ballyhoo rides much farther forward in the bait than in most lures. Remember, dolphin, like most fish, almost always swallow their food headfirst. That means when they grab a trolled ballyhoo from behind, they often bite it behind the hook and must turn the bait around to eat it. That's when you separate the men from the boys in the cockpit.

Dropping a bait back is really no more than stopping it in its tracks so the fish can turn it and eat it headfirst. When I teach bait rigging at *Florida Sportsman* shows, I always get asked about double-hooking ballyhoo. "We went out last week and all the fish were short striking. We needed a trailer hook in our baits. They were just eating tails today."

I have a hard time believing a self-respecting dolphin ever wakes up and decides to only eat tails today! I'm convinced a fish striking the back end of a bait is either too small to eat the bait whole or is trying to disable the bait to eat headfirst. It's the angler's responsibility to make this happen, thus recreating what happens in nature every day.

Monofilament leaders are important for successful dropbacks. It's far more difficult for a fish to turn a bait or grab it headfirst on a wire leader than on mono.

When we're trolling ballyhoo for dolphin, every line is rigged through a release clip somewhere on the boat. If the line doesn't run through an outrigger pin, we'll run it through a clip on the

> **Dropping a bait back is really no more than stopping it in its tracks so the fish can turn it and eat it headfirst.**

transom of the boat. If no rigger pins are available, wrapping one end of a piece of copper rigging wire around the rod butt and the other end lightly around your main line will get the job done. Just pull the main line from the rodtip down to the butt and wrap the copper wire once around. It should release on the strike.

Unlike sailfish, dolphin rarely act like they're in slow motion. You certainly don't want to troll with your reels out of gear or barely engaged. Be ready to act fast when you see that forehead piercing the surface. Once you see a dolphin closing in on your bait, it's pretty much committed. My experience has been to go ahead and get the reel out of gear and the bait free-falling into the fish's mouth. If you can stop the bait in the water, and let him grab it headfirst, you're usually home free. The trick is keeping just enough thumb pressure to keep the reel from backlashing while still letting the bait tumble down the dolphin's throat. We don't use clickers while natural bait trolling. My experience is most clickers put too much pressure on the reel spool; they don't let the bait come to a complete stop on the dropback.

When most fishermen feel a fish grab the bait and start moving off with it, they make the mistake of throwing the reel in gear and "setting the hook." The problem is, they feel the line starting to peel off, and they assume the fish must be moving away from the boat. A dolphin doesn't know where you are or what you're up to. Chances are it's moving in a direction other than straight away from the boat. That means there's slack line, and when you jerk you won't be setting the hook in anything

but slack. Just because the line is heating up your thumb, it can just as easily be water pressure on slack line while your fish is swimming perpendicular to the boat. The best (and only) correct thing to do when a dolphin starts swimming away with your bait after a dropback is reel as fast as you can. You can do a much better job of setting today's ultra-sharp ballyhoo hooks by reeling fast than by jerking the rod.

Fighting

I've been very fortunate in my angling career. I've caught all the Atlantic billfish (except spearfish, which are sissies and don't count), but the toughest fight I ever had was from a 53-pound dolphin, hooked on a spinning rod. Even female dolphin have a tall enough forehead to use to their advantage when you're trying to get them within gaff range.

A kingfish or wahoo may be faster, but when they're done running, they're done. A dolphin on the other hand will run and jump with the best of them. But when they run out of gas, they can turn their head broadside to you and make it far more

Putting a fighting belt on a lady angler. She needs to raise her rodtip and let it do the work.

difficult to get them to the boat. For the angler, fighting a dolphin is a matter of steady pressure. Grab a few inches when you can. As all big-fish fights go, gaining line on a big dolphin is about pumping the rod with very short strokes and taking up whatever line you can on the down-stroke.

It's the captain that matters once a dolphin is hooked. If you're reeling in all your lines once you've got a big fish hooked, you're going to get consistently outfished by other boats. You want your best baits in the water when you're on the

fish. Well guess what? If you've got a fish on, you're pretty much on the fish. Keep fishing!

Keeping your lines in the water when you've got a fish on can be accomplished by turning the boat to keep the hooked dolphin amidships and clear of the other baits. Dolphin fights often necesssitate a mate popping out an outrigger or moving some lines around, but the captain should keep the boat moving forward. It accomplishes two important things. It not only keeps pressure on the hooked fish, it keeps the other baits fishing. Only when

you're in serious danger of running out of line, or the fish absolutely can't be pulled alongside, should the boat go out of gear.

Landing

More dolphin are lost at the gaff than any other time after hookup. It's unnecessary and shouldn't happen more than once in a bluemoon. They've got a perfect target with that big, wide head. If you're ready, that bull will be in the box before he has a chance to react.

As the fish is worked closer to the boat, he'll be easier to control when the boat is moving forward. When the pressure on a fish is constant, it's far more difficult for him to turn his head and reverse his direction. Secondly, a long wind-on leader means you can put extra pressure during the last few yards. This is no place to be timid! Grab the leader and take control. The more you let him get his head, the more trouble you'll have.

Never try to gaff a fish behind the boat. Not only is the propwash messing up your view of the fish, it's also giving you a horrible angle to gaff from. It's much easier to hit a fish moving parallel to the boat instead of straight at you. The clean, non-turbulent water alongside the boat provides a better view and a much better angle to gaff from.

Oversize landing nets (left) are becoming more popular for fish you may want to release.

Grabbing the leader too close to the fish can result in a fish shaking off; better almost to lift the fish with the rod.

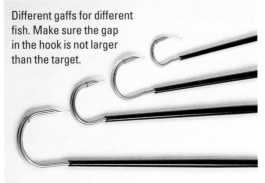

Different gaffs for different fish. Make sure the gap in the hook is not larger than the target.

Never reach out with a gaff unless you've got a plan. Make sure you can *easily* reach him. Make sure the gaff is behind the leader. I've seen some beautiful fish lost because the gaff man got the leader wrapped around the gaff. If you reach ahead of the leader, and the fish flops or changes direction, the line is wrapped around the gaff and the fish is gone. Most gaff shots are lost because somebody got impatient and lunged at the fish. If your gaff is sharp, it's all about a fluid, steady motion. Don't try to reach too far; make sure your feet are spread. You must be firmly planted to the deck. Your gaff shot needs to be one fluid motion from the water to the fish box. If you keep him coming, you'll be in control.

think about how much freeboard your boat has and whether you have a top over the cockpit. If you're a light-tackle fisherman and you gaff 6- to 8- pound dolphin, make sure you have a gaff with no larger than a 2-inch hook. You'll want to be able to reach a fish you've worked alongside. Trust me, the shorter and stouter the gaff, the easier the fish is to control.

Be safe. Rods have to be out of the nearby holders; there can't be any hooks or teasers on the deck. If you're in a center console, make sure you're going to be clear of the T-top once you start bringing the fish aboard. Make very sure you know where you're going to put the 'phin. Open the fish box. Remember, once the fish is gaffed, "He who hesitates is lost."

Cobia and dolphin are tied near the top of the list of fish that can hurt you the most if they get off the gaff in the cockpit. Unless the fish is small enough to control easily, get the fish in the fish box first and worry about your rig later. If a big dolphin gets loose in your cockpit, the best-case scenario is you'll be finding blood stains six months later in places you never thought of scrubbing. More likely you'll be cutting your day short because somebody got whacked or got a hook thrown in their leg. **SB**

> Here he comes. Slide that bull into the box and slam the lid on him.

Use one motion from the gaff to the waiting fish box. A thrashing dolphin in the cockpit spells trouble.

Tournament kingfish fishermen were the first ones I ever saw using 12-and even 14-foot gaffs. They may be great for kings, but if you've ever been beaten up by an 8-foot gaff when you couldn't control a 30-pound dolphin, you'll see why an 8-foot gaff is as long as we ever use.

To determine what size gaff is best for you,

Bad angle (top): Mate can't gaff a fish coming straight at boat. Perfect shot (middle): Fish is broadside, with the boat moving forward. Gaff is behind the leader. Dolphin under control (bottom).

Have a Plan

- Never gaff a fish behind the boat.

- Gaff fish while it's moving parallel with the boat.

- Make sure the gaff is behind the leader.

- Don't try to gaff the fish from underneath.

- Don't reach too far.

- One fluid motion from water to fish box.

- Aim for the fattest part of the shoulder. Restrain a dolphin's head for the best control.

CHAPTER 15

Dolphin on The Calendar

One of the truly majestic aspects of offshore fishing is experiencing the global movements of gamefish populations. A dolphin may travel 100 miles in a single day.

How funny is it, with the kind of frequent-flier miles dolphin rack up, that we all take off on Saturday morning thinking we'll find the same school of dolphin we hit on Tuesday? A dolphin doesn't know where it is, and it doesn't care. It's looking for the right isotherm (area of pre-ferred water temperature), the next meal and maybe a sweet young bull. A dolphin's travels will take it thousands of miles, but where the fish will be next month is predictable. Let's look at the calendar and see if we can figure out where the fish will be and when.

A dolphin's travels will span thousands of miles, but where the fish shows up next month is predictable.

The size and number of these beauties points to the Pacific coast of Central America, in this case Crocodile Bay, Costa Rica.

The Four Seasons

E ach month of the year brings a different set of circumstances to any marine environment. Wind direction, current and dominant food sources change. Dolphin react to changes in the seasons; it's only us anglers who get

The loners of winter are usually big bulls.

> **Dolphin have learned to change with the seasons. It's only us anglers that get confused.**

confused when confronted with new and different conditions.

Remember, there are essentially two populations of dolphin: one above the equator and one below. For simplicity's sake, it's true that the closer to the equator, the longer the good dolphin season will run.

Winter, Spring, Summer and Fall

In the winter, dolphin are harder to find throughout most of their range, but when you get a bite it's usually a great fish.

Spring is simply the greatest time of all for dolphin fishermen. There are big fish on the rips, and the weather can be perfect for days at a time. No dolphin fisherman would schedule his wedding during May—unless it included a fishing honeymoon.

As the big fish come closer to shore, they bring the babies with them. The lazy days of summer are all about schoolies and catching dolphin on light tackle within sight of land.

The cool winds of fall send the fish offshore and south. Trolling can really be slow, but one of the most beautiful sights on earth occurs when migrating "green hornets" get a bait pod bunched up.

For most of the dolphin's range, you're looking at a minimum of an eight-month fishery per year. Heck, it takes me four months to make enough leaders to resume the battle.

Equatorial waters may produce big fish all year.

With the great runs of spring, these fish could be found almost anywhere.

If this little guy showed shallower than 80 feet, chances are it was during the fall.

Winter

During winter, no matter the hemisphere, dolphin are most abundant in the equatorial zone. The equatorial zone is simply a narrow band of warm water that extends roughly 20 percent north and south from the equator, where the water's always warm and dolphin fishing can be good year-round.

During the northern hemisphere winter season, there can still be excellent dolphin fishing off South Florida, the southern Gulf of Mexico and the Caribbean, as warm southerly winds develop

Off the U.S. coasts, dolphin fishing can be tied year-round to the proximity of warm blue water.

between cold fronts. When the wind comes from the east and southeast, it will push warm, blue water into the colder, murkier water caused by the counter-current. This will set up excellent dolphin conditions.

Farther up the east coast, and in the mid- to northern Gulf, dolphin fishing success is directly dependent on the proximity of the warm bluewater currents.

In Northeast Florida we catch dolphin in the winter, but it's dependant on a sharp temperature break. If cold water out to the edge of the continental shelf mixes with warm-water pushes inshore of 1,200 feet, we'll often see some of the biggest bulls of the year cruising the rip.

A rack of spinners means schoolies are in the plan.

As February and March come around, dolphin start riding the currents north along the Atlantic Coast. Big dolphin, most of which have spawned in the warm tropics, will start riding the spinoffs and eddies first. Once again, the northerly wind may inspire sails and kings, but it's the warmer southerly breezes between cold fronts that push the migration north. Northerly winds generally occur regularly this

time of year, often about a week apart. This can make for very challenging conditions for dolphin fishermen, but a week or more of southerly breezes can make for a great bite.

Similar local weather conditions also make dolphin fishing productive in antipodal latitudes. If you're heading somewhere exotic, check with local operators about weather and currents that affect dolphin fishing locally, regardless of season.

Warm, tropical Pacific waters bring slammers in any month. El Salvador anglers show evidence.

Spring

As the cold fronts begin to spread out and lose their intensity, dolphin start to make up a bigger percentage of the sportfishing catches along the southeast and mid-Atlantic coasts of the United States. The population gets bigger and the average-size fish gets smaller as the new crop of schoolies, only a few months old, joins the procession north.

April and May evidence both an east-west and north-south migration. May is the best dolphin month just about everywhere. From The Bahamas through the Keys, in the Gulf and on up to Georgia and the Carolinas, dolphin fishermen wish they had two months of May and no February.

Real dolphin anglers wish they had two months of May and no February!

In May, the northerly winds are rare and short-lived. The rips are usually close enough to the coast for most boats to reach, but not so far inshore the dolphin don't follow them. The reason May stands out is as much about water temperatures and wind direction as it is about dolphin populations. In the upper half of the dolphin's range, the warmer (over 77 degrees) water is reachable, but the colder water inshore means the fish are usually concentrated near the temperature breaks. The breaks become easier to find and move closer to shore as the prevailing breezes start to settle into a southeast pattern. Look for similar conditions in spring throughout the world.

High seas may call for big boats in spring, but the rewards are usually worth it.

The easterly breezes of spring brought this beauty within sight of the South Florida skyline.

Summary

June and July provide plenty of small dolphin hopping around the rips closer to shore. In Northeast Florida, you'll catch about as many dolphin in June as in May, but the smaller schoolies start to take over. The bigger fish push toward the northern end of the range and pull farther offshore with the Gulf Stream. The weather is usually delightful. The northern Gulf of Mexico also begins to experience better dolphin fishing than the Atlantic side.

Weedlines are easy to find on the prevailing southeast winds, but they won't all have dolphin on them. You may have to do some searching, or stay with a healthy chunk of sargassum and drift live baits under it until the fish show up.

In the Gulf of Mexico there's only so far north the fish can go since the shallow continental shelf extends so far out to sea. The major push of big fish has left Northeast Florida by July 1, which is about the same time fish in the Gulf will reach the north end of their range. That's a good time to fish out of any port of call from Panama City, Florida to Port Arthur, Texas. It lasts through the summer.

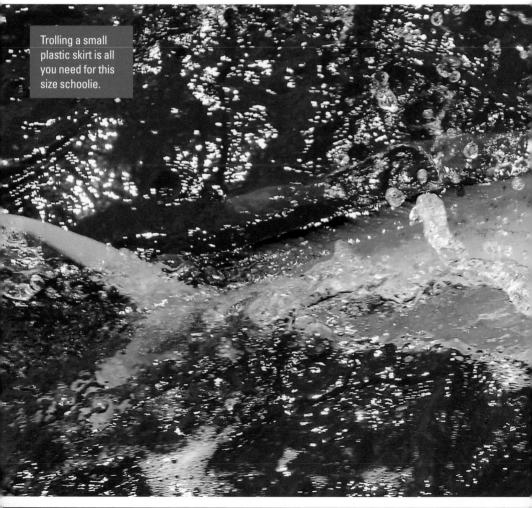

Trolling a small plastic skirt is all you need for this size schoolie.

Midsummer "grasshopper," below the minimum size for some waters.

Fall

On the U.S. Atlantic Coast, something strange seems to happen to dolphin between August 1 and October 1. It may be the preponderance of bait in shallow water, or it may be because they know winter is coming, but every big dolphin I've ever seen feeding in 60 feet of water or less has been in the late summer and early fall. If you find a log, or just about anything that's been floating a while, there's a good chance

Fall will often mean dolphin in shallower water than at any other time of year.

it'll hold nice fish, even if it's closer inshore than you're used to catching dolphin. Let a tropical storm flush some heavy timber into the Gulf Stream, and let the southeast wind push it inshore, and you'll score perfect run-and-gun conditions.

Once the water cools substantially, dolphin start pushing back south. Most southeastern U.S. anglers catch nice dolphin while looking for sailfish. You will often find dolphin in pursuit of bait balls right alongside sailfish. The fish are totally locked in on feeding. If the bait schools are bunched up, the dolphin will be chasing them. Sometimes, during this period of the year, you find fish moving intently on a southern migration. These fish can be very difficult to catch if you're not in the vicinity of bait. SB

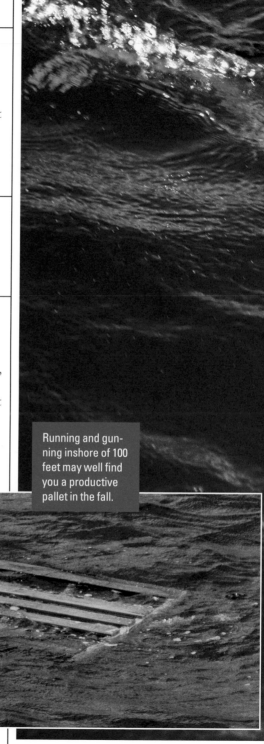

Running and gunning inshore of 100 feet may well find you a productive pallet in the fall.

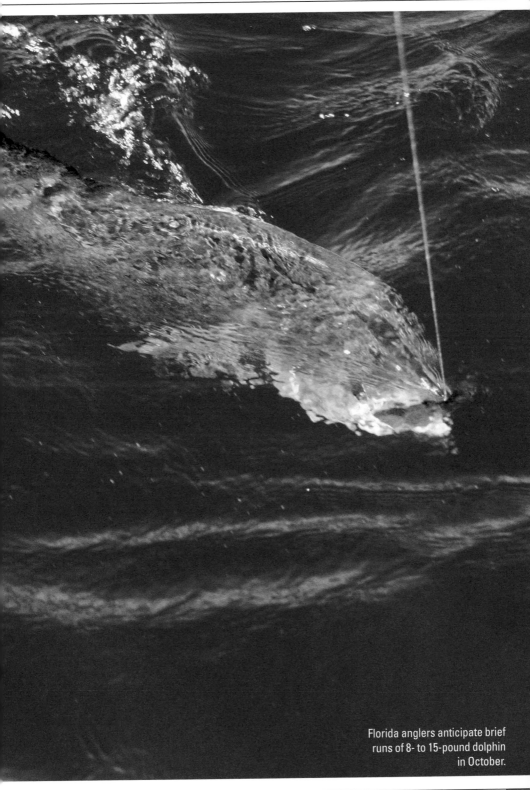

Florida anglers anticipate brief runs of 8- to 15-pound dolphin in October.

CHAPTER 16

Environmental Factors

Dolphin are very sensitive to environmental changes. Wind direction, water temperature, water clarity and the direction and strength of the current all factor into the equation.

Years ago, we knew little about surface temperatures or currents. When we loaded up for dolphin and came home with empty fish boxes, we explained it away as the "They Ain't Biting" phenomenon. We've much to discover, but fortunately, scientists and anglers have learned a great deal about the ocean over the last 20 years. Technology is also making it easier to predict ocean conditions before you leave the dock.

Dolphin are very adaptable, but they prefer the clear, warm waters of the open sea. Now we're learning that there are often environmental factors that determine the success of a day's fishing. Let's look at some reasons why they are, or are not, biting.

Dolphin are very adaptable, but they prefer the clear, warm waters of the open sea.

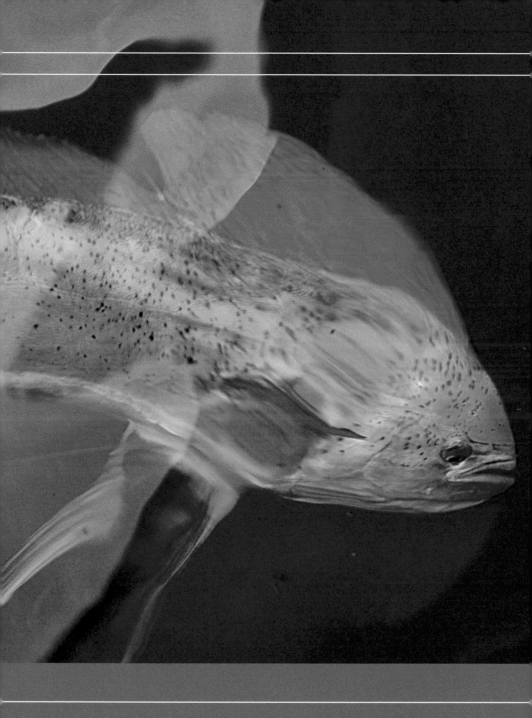

Among the Gulf Stream's gifts: the sight of a lit-up dolphin in unforgettable blue water.

Winds

Fishermen are hard to please. We want wind, but not too much. You'll catch fish on slick days, but light winds offer better conditions. Wind stirs the water and cools the surface. Even though we've learned that dolphin occasionally dive more than 300 feet, they spend most of their time in the upper 100 feet of the water column. A little breeze can keep them hunting on top.

Flat days sure aren't a reason to stay home. Dolphin fishermen actually fare better than a lot of fishermen on slick days. Tuna fishing usually crashes when the sun is high in the sky, and you catch more wahoo on cloudy, choppy days. Look at their eyes. Tuna, wahoo and swordfish have big eyes high on their heads. Dolphin have smaller eyes on the side of the head. They can tolerate

The tip of a dolphin's dorsal piercing the water's surface sure looks great on a calm day.

The same northerly winds sailfis

a calm, bright ocean surface in conditions that would singe the eyeballs of other species. Still, better fishing generally occurs with a little chop to cool the water, stir up the bait and make hooks and leaders less discernible. Flat days can be a little slow, but they sure beat hanging on or crawling around the cockpit in a 20-knot north wind. As

Capt. George LaBonte of Jupiter, Florida, is fond of saying, "It never gets too calm to scare me."

Wind direction is one of the key factors influencing dolphin fishing success. When the calendar says early spring, and the northerly migration begins, the number of days bringing easterly wind will determine when the dolphin run occurs on the east coast of the United States. If there's a sustained southwesterly wind early in the season, dolphin are far more likely to migrate up the eastern wall of the Gulf Stream, largely out of reach unless approached from The Bahamas.

Even if weeks of easterly winds have warmed the water, a southerly wind combined with a northerly

Scanning the surface for signs of dolphin is easier the calmer it gets.

shermen love can make times tough for dolphin hunters.

Gulf Stream current will bunch up the weeds and bait. Weedlines generally run in a south/southwest to a north/northeast direction. When the current is pushing to the north, and the breeze is from the southeast, you'll usually find the best rips.

If the wind clocks around from the north, it becomes more difficult to find surface features. Dolphin are more scattered and generally not as aggressive. The same northerly winds sailfish fishermen love can make things very difficult for dolphin hunters.

You also need to understand the difference in wind direction, as it applies to sea conditions. A 15-knot northerly wind working against a 5-knot

Gulf Stream current produces a much nastier ocean than a 15-knot southerly wind in the same waters, for instance.

Along much of the U.S. east coast, southwesterly wind can provide defined rip lines and good action on a daily basis, but can spell real trouble if it stays too long. A longterm southwesterly wind will push the warm surf water offshore, and pull up the colder water off the bottom to take its place, thus "turning over" the water. Let this upwelling condition persist long enough, and you'll be trolling in water too cold for a dolphin to tolerate. The Gulf Stream will get pushed out too far for most boats to reach.

It was ideal conditions for these anglers (note the perfect gaff shot, from the top through the shoulder).

Tides and Currents

Tides and currents are the roads dolphin travel on. When winter's on the way, some dolphin swim into the current to find their way back to the tropics. As the winter wanes, they reverse route and follow the Gulf Stream back to the north. The Gulf Stream is a river that winds through the western North Atlantic Ocean. It begins with the easterly trade winds near the equator. The winds move the water, and the movement to the north begins. Numerous currents from the Caribbean and the Gulf of Mexico merge to form the Gulf Stream, which moves up the east coast of North America. The Stream is generally 35 to 45 miles wide, and averages 1.5 to 4 knots as it pushes north. With an average water temp of 79 degrees, it is home sweet home to most of the western North Atlantic dolphin population.

Associated with the Gulf Stream are smaller eddies and counter currents that spin off from the main flow. It's these counter currents that keep dedicated dolphin hunters staring at their computers. When a warm, well-defined spinoff approaches the continental shelf in the spring, it's time to call in sick to work.

Some anglers get very excited when the Gulf Stream moves close to land, warming the inshore waters. In my experience,

this is not the best time to fish. Once the stream gets inshore of the continental shelf, fish may spread out over a massive area. If the inshore water is too cold for dolphin until you reach the edge of the continental shelf, guess where the bait and fish are going to be stacked?

Tide can be very important in dolphin fishing, particularly if you live where there's deep blue water within 20 miles of a major inlet. When the tide starts falling out of an inlet, the river water spreads offshore. Dream dolphin conditions occur when a falling tide hits an onshore wind, and the

The Gulf Stream is generally 35 to 45 miles wide, with typically 1.4 to 4 knots of current pushing north.

Even though this sport-fisherman appears motionless, the Gulf Stream may be pushing him north at 4 knots.

bait and weed are trapped in the conflict. For the most part, the major impact of daily tides is felt closest to the inlets. If you're one of the lucky souls who live where a major waterway feeds into the ocean, and blue water is close, daily tides are a huge factor in your dolphin catch. Learn to be in the area when a falling tide rip reaches the blue water between 100 and 300 feet.

Winds, tides and currents are all major factors in making up good dolphin conditions. Look for 79-degree blue water with a strong current and some good rips. Learning when and how to find these conditions is what make good fishermen great. **SB**

> **Tides can be very important in dolphin fishing, particularly if you live where there's blue water within 20 miles of an inlet.**

Tides pushing out of an inlet can set up a dream dolphin scenario.

The same weather that causes
squally conditions can trigger a
bite. Just don't stay too long.

CHAPTER 17

Q&A

With regional experts

We all know a fisherman who catches so many more big fish, he seems to be on another plane. The captains who always are in position when the bite is on. Do they have a sixth sense? Or is it a secret bait, maybe an unknown satellite service that tells them exactly where to fish?

More likely, it's a hundred little things that start in the rigging of their boats, and cover every aspect of their rods, reels, bait and tackle.

Let's spend a few minutes with some of the best from these three regions.

Capt. Robert Johnson Northeast Florida

Capt. Brett Holden Freeport, Texas

Capt. Bouncer Smith South Florida

We all know a fisherman who catches so many more big fish, he seems to be on another plane.

Successful South Florida captain Bouncer Smith with a beautiful fly-caught dolphin.

Captain Robert Johnson has few equals when it comes to catching big dolphin.

Regional Expert:
CAPT. ROBERT JOHNSON
Northeast Florida

Captain Robert Johnson has no equals among Northeast Florida dolphin fishermen. His *Jodie Lynn II* is always in the right place when the bite is on. His methods and philosophies are well worth emulating.

SB: Anyone with the pressure of having a paying charter on board has to have a system for finding the fish. What conditions are you looking for to fish for dolphin?

Johnson: The most important thing I'm looking for is any kind of change. A temperature change and a current break usually happen together. The fish will be on a break, even if you can't easily see it.

SB: What about weeds? Do you have to find them to find fish?

Johnson: Bait is more important. You can fish the biggest weedline in the ocean, but if there's no bait, there's no reason for dolphin to be there. You may pick up a fish here and there, but all the best days have three things in common: They all have a temperature break, accompanied by a tide rip, with lots of bait hiding in the weeds.

SB: It seems everything's changed since satellite pictures came on the screen. Do you use them?

Johnson: Of course I use them, but you have to be careful. Here in Northeast Florida we run an average of 50 miles before we start trolling. If I look at a picture taken at 3 a.m., conditions have 6 hours to change before I get to the spot I saw on my computer. I pay more attention to which

"We always keep our lines in the water. The best time to get a strike is when you already have a fish on."

way a temperature break is moving than trying to pinpoint where it was. You'll usually find your best temperature breaks are farther offshore early in the spring. I'll often fish as deep as 1,200 feet early in the season, but later on the rips usually appear closer to shore, say between 120 and 300 feet. The "engines" that drive the rips always seem to work from southeast to northwest. If a rip is in 800 feet south of the inlet today, there's a good chance it'll be north of the inlet tomorrow in 150 feet.

SB: Here's something many of us struggle with: You find the conditions you want, but the fish aren't biting. How long do you stay with it?

Johnson: It depends on my charter. If they're willing to hang in there, I'll often stay on the same rip for 3 hours without a bite, if the conditions look good. I've dragged through the same rip for a half-day without a strike, only to see them suddenly turn on.

SB: You're primarily a natural-bait fisherman. Can you beat a ballyhoo for dolphin?

Johnson: I don't think so. A naked, mono-rigged ballyhoo is my all-time favorite. I'll put a Sea Witch or other small lure in front of the ballyhoo to help it hold together and stay in the water, but I'm not a big lure guy.

SB: Do you pull mono because you get more bites on mono or because you get a better hook-up ratio?

Johnson: Yes. Yes, we get more bites, and yes, we get better hookups.

SB: I've seen you rack up huge catches of big dolphin. What's the secret to catching double-digits of big fish in a day?

Johnson: First off, I start the track feature on my chartplotter as soon as we start fishing. Once I get a strike, I'm relentless about staying on top of that spot. Second, we fish either an 8- or a 9-line spread.

When a school of dolphin arrives, it's sometimes best to stop the boat and get the whole crew in the action.

The baits are always in the water. Once we hook a fish, I'll turn the boat in the direction he's moving, clear any lines he may cross, but we always keep [other lines] in the water. The best time to get a strike is when you've already got a fish on. Third, my boat idles at a little over 7 knots. That's a little faster than most boats' trolling speed and eliminates some of the smaller fish. I also pull larger-size ballyhoo.

Regional Expert:
CAPT. BRETT HOLDEN
Freeport, Texas

Captain Brett Holden runs the *The Booby Trap*, a 46-foot Bertram Express out of Freeport, Texas. He's a bluewater junkie and lives to troll for dolphin, wahoo and marlin. Fishing in the Gulf benefits from plenty of manmade structure.

Captain Brett Holden with a slammer caught near an oil rig. Gulf of Mexico anglers have thousands of rigs that attract everything that swims.

SB: Brett, what time of year do you guys start fishing for dolphin?

Holden: We really don't see a lot of dolphin before May and our peak is in July. The small dolphin will be all over the rips offshore of our rivermouths, often within 20 miles of shore during summer. The big offshore fish stretch from late May until the water cools in the fall.

SB: Where do you start looking for dolphin?

Holden: I'm looking for current rips and weedlines from 180 feet out. Any area where there's a big change in bottom structure and depth will have a corresponding rip somewhere nearby. Keep in mind we have many rivers that pour into the Gulf off Texas. There's almost always logs or some kind of trash we can fish on.

SB: What about oil rigs?

Holden: We're covered in oil rigs. We fish the rigs and the crew boats tied to them from 300 to 1,000 feet. Most of the rigs deeper than that are floating rigs, but they also hold fish. Crew boats tied to the rigs all day will almost always hold big dolphin. We caught a box full of 20- to 46-pound dolphin last weekend out from under the crew boats tied to the rigs.

SB: What's your spread like when you're fishing for dolphin?

Holden: I'm a ballyhoo fisherman. We almost always catch our biggest dolphin on Ilander-and-ballyhoo or naked ballyhoo. We pull some marlin lures in our spreads, but the standard Ilander-and-ballyhoo draws the most strikes from wahoo and dolphin. We also have excellent wahoo fishing. It's not unusual for us to catch 10 to 20 wahoo in a day.

SB: When there's wahoo around, do you fish wire leaders?

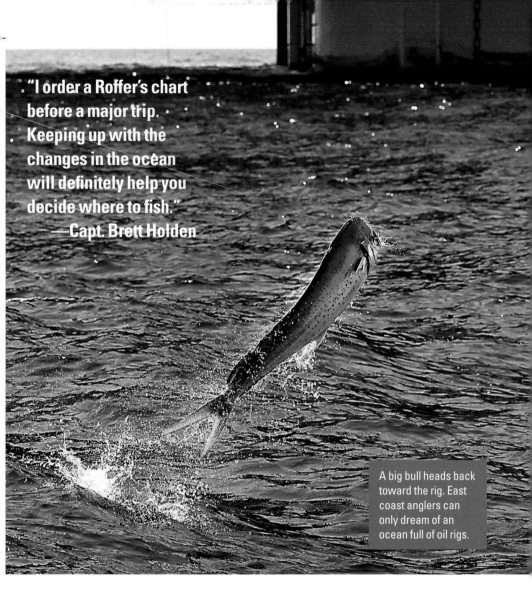

"I order a Roffer's chart before a major trip. Keeping up with the changes in the ocean will definitely help you decide where to fish."
— Capt. Brett Holden

A big bull heads back toward the rig. East coast anglers can only dream of an ocean full of oil rigs.

Holden: Not unless I have to. I think we get more bites on mono. I think we get a much better hookup ratio with mono. Unless we're specifically targeting wahoo, I stick with mono.

SB: What about teasers?

Holden: I don't use them. I only pull 5 lines. I'd much rather be able to control the chaos that a bunch of big dolphin can create. Five lines are enough to handle without having to worry about teasers.

SB: How fast do you troll?

Holden: When we're marlin fishing, we're trolling upward of 8 knots. When we troll for dolphin, we pull more natural baits and drop the speed to 6 to 7.5 knots. We catch dolphin both ways. But when dolphin are the target, we'll troll ballyhoo, and they just swim better between 6 and 7.5 knots. If we find a great piece of surface structure, like a football field-size weed patch, we'll chum and drift bait chunks.

SB: With as far as you need to run, do you pay much attention to satellite pictures?

Holden: Everyday, I constantly monitor buoy weather and satellite pictures. I'll order a ROFFS chart before a major trip. Keeping up with the changes in the ocean will definitely help you decide where to fish.

Captain Bouncer Smith has guided many a young angler to their first big dolphin.

Regional Expert:
CAPT. BOUNCER SMITH
South Florida

Nobody in South Florida has more salt water in their veins than Capt. Bouncer Smith. He's the captain of *Bouncer's Dusky* and he says dolphin are on a 12-month calendar in South Florida.

SB: Bouncer, break down your calendar for me a little. What time of year do you target big fish versus looking for groups of schooling fish?

Smith: In January and February, we'll see two classes of dolphin. We'll either see very small fish, some of them not even legal, or we'll see the occasional very big fish. By the time March rolls around, any time we get a strong east wind with a strong northerly current, there's a very good chance of catching big dolphin on our kite baits. They'll be mixed with good numbers of sailfish. Sometimes the 15- to 40-pound fish can literally wear you out.

By the time we reach May, we're still catching big dolphin, but the schoolies are getting thicker. In June, it's almost all schooling fish ranging from barely legal up to about 6 pounds. In July, they're getting a little bigger and moving farther offshore to escape the hot water. I believe dolphin prefer water from 75 to 80 degrees. Once it gets up around 82 they will head offshore to deeper, cooler water.

In August and September, the schoolies have reached 5 to 10 pounds, but are really hit or miss. With the first few cold fronts of October, the fish start moving back closer to shore, but they still range between 5 and 15 pounds. In November and December, we're back to catching pretty good fish on our kites, but most of them are still under 15 pounds.

SB: Bouncer, you've mentioned you spend time kite fishing. Do you also fish a natural bait spread for dolphin?

Smith: No, I fish a spread of high-speed lures, including one really big lure to act as a teaser or in case we run across a blue marlin. But I need to be ready to run in case we spot birds or something floating. I can't chase birds without tearing up natural baits, so I stick to lures. That way I don't have to reel the lines in when I need to get going in a hurry.

SB: You seem to put a lot of emphasis on spotting fish, then running to them. What percentage of your fish do you "run-and-gun" or spot first, versus those you troll up?

Smith: We probably catch 80 percent of our dolphin off something floating or under birds. But some of the biggest fish will come from the middle of nowhere on the troll.

SB: South Florida seems to be the epicenter of kite fishing. What are your favorite baits for dolphin on the kite?

Smith: Herring are my go-to bait. I also like big cigar minnows. The days I really love are when we've got enough breeze to slow-troll a bait spread on one side of a weedline, yet keep the kite in the air on the other

side. If you rig a ballyhoo with the hook just in front of his head (or hook him through the lips) and keep his head out of the water, you can troll the thickest weeds around without getting snagged. Having just the tail of the bait touching the water drives big dolphin nuts. Sometimes we'll just drag a rubber skirt, with the hook out of the water. It's a deadly method when everybody else is battling the weeds. **SB**

Bouncer's dream day has frigates flying over a rip and enough breeze to slow-troll one side, kite fish the other (below).

CHAPTER 18

Research:
The Key to the Future

We can fuss all we want about having to "take a lawyer fishing with you" to understand fishing regulations, but the results of most management measures have been overwhelmingly positive. Such measures largely depend on quality research. One shudders to think about the likely decimation of such species as redfish, swordfish, sailfish, king mackerel, red snapper and goliath grouper had it not been for the efforts of the fisheries research community and the recreational fishing community.

Because they are so highly migratory, dolphin are more difficult to manage than most coastal pelagic, reef or estuarine species. It may well take international cooperation to sustain healthy dolphin stocks. We still have much to learn about their spawning and migration habits, and without that knowledge it is difficult to manage any species.

We still have much to learn about dolphin migrations and spawning patterns. Without that knowledge, it's hard to manage any species.

See DVD for more on dolphin conservation.

Only by remaining
vigilant on a global
scale can we ensure
there will be plenty
when she's taller
than her dolphin.

Handle with Care

Many anglers contend that the minimum for dolphin should be raised to 22 or 24 inches and the bag cut to 7 per angler.

Good dolphin fishing may seem as certain as tomorrow's sunrise.

Isn't this one fish, at least, that we don't have to worry about being depleted?

Well, yes, to some extent that's true. You can count on hordes of dolphin, or mahi mahi, turning up in countless places next year all through the deep warm seas.

And yet their migrating aggregations can make them prime targets for industrial overfishing as some more traditional catches are caught out. The name mahi is popularized more and more by the seafood industry—first in Hawaii, but now everywhere that the mild popular meat hits the commercial scales.

The jury apparently is out on whether today's dolphin stocks are holding steady, declining or possibly improving.

At any rate, we should consider them fragile and in potential danger.

In the 1990s, commercial longliners were testing Atlantic waters, and the strength of their fish holds, taking ton after ton of dolphin. Some boats labored under loads of 28,000 pounds and more.

At the same time, several enterprising firms were cranking up to collect sargassum weed to make an industrial product. The great mats of sargassum happen to be prime habitat for dolphin, and home to endless marine animals such as juvenile fish and crustaceans.

Thanks largely to protests of sportfishing conservationists, the dolphin long-lining and sargassum scheme were mostly thwarted.

Some tighter catch limits have been adopted. In the prime dolphin waters of the Florida and Georgia Atlantic coast, the recreational size limit is 20 inches minimum (fork length) with an individual bag limit of 10 as

Not only are we going to have to make sure dolphin stocks remain healthy, we must continue to protect sargassum, which has an impact on countless species.

part of a boat maximum of 60. Commercial takes require licensing and the same 20-inch minimum.

A 20-inch dolphin is barely of spawning size. Many anglers contend that the minimum size limit should be raised to 22 or 24 inches and the bag cut to seven. That size length may be reasonable because peanuts yield very small fillets anyway. Let them grow a bit, perhaps, which they do in a hurry, adding inches in weeks.

An average-size female dolphin will spawn a quarter-million drifting eggs, while a 43-inch fish will drop several million.

Let's do everything we can to enjoy these colorful and delectable characters while making sure they are always plentiful.

There have been almost no comprehensive stock assessments of dolphin. But one study in the southern Caribbean warned years ago that that an overfishing problem could catch fishermen by surprise because excess pressure could be directed at visible dolphin stocks even as they are steadily depleted.

That's a surprise we don't need. **SB**

Many developing nations depend on healthy dolphin populations to fuel their economy as well as feed their people. Fisheries managers face a tough job, keeping subsistence fishermen going, while keeping large-scale commercial harvesters from impacting the dolphin population. As with so many stressed fisheries, a sustainable population of dolphin has to be the primary focus.

CHAPTER 19

From the Gaff To Your Table

Dolphin aren't bloody enough to require bleeding, but they do have to be carefully handled to live up to their delicious reputation. Taking care of your dolphin is vital; it starts as soon as the 'phin comes aboard and ends on the skillet.

Fish bruise just like you do. A bruise is nothing more than a place where blood rushes to the site of a wound, and it's blood that makes a piece of fish taste strong. The next time you're on a bite of schoolies, don't unhook each one and drop it on the deck. As delicately as possible, put the fish into a bed of finely crushed ice or seawater slush in your fish box.

Fish bruise just like you do. A bruise is nothing more than blood rushing to the site of a wound, and it's blood that makes a fish taste strong.

DOLPHIN

See DVD BONUS FEATURES for more on filleting, cleaning and cooking your catch.

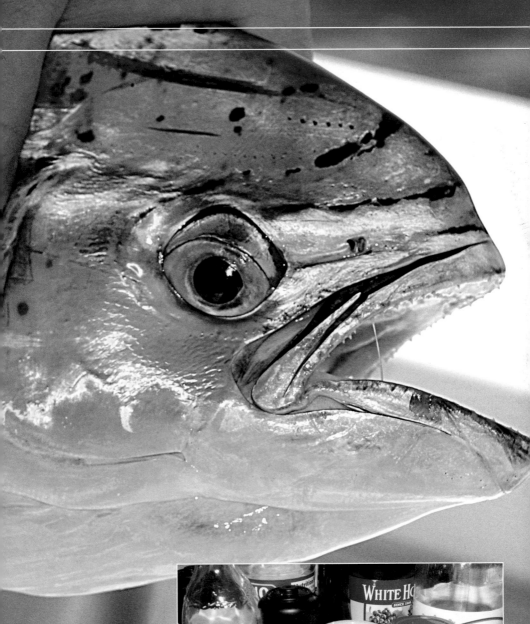

When the dolphin bite is on, you'll need lots of different spices. Eating dolphin while they're fresh is always best.

Ice is Nice

If you plan on fishing regularly, purchasing an ice machine that generates crushed ice may be a wise investment. Most commercial fishermen use crushed ice because it can be mixed into a salt-water slurry that drops the temperature in the fish

box a few degrees. The mix lasts longer, too. On our boat, no fish hits the deck if we can help it. A dolphin goes straight into the box, which will have too much ice in it to give the fish much room to bang around. From the biggest wahoo to the smallest sea bass, our fish are unhooked and tucked into the ice.

When it's time to head home, especially with a long run ahead, it's a good idea to pull out your

At the Cleaning Table

All fish taste better if you cut out the

Chilled fish are much easier to fillet, and the final product tastes better.

It's amazing to me how some fish can taste so different depending on their size. Wahoo, for example, taste the same whether your fish weighed 15 or 80 pounds. Swordfish are the same way; so are mako sharks and sea bass. Grouper get coarse and grainy when they get big. So do kingfish, cobia, drum—and dolphin. The next time you catch a 50-pound bull, and your buddy catches a 15-pounder, be a pal and trade him. Let him tell you what a great guy you are, and then snicker under your breath all the way home.

It's just like Grandpa said, "You've got to have the right tools to do the job right." In cleaning a fish

properly, the right knife is vitally important. Of course it has to come sharp and be easy to keep sharp. My favorite blade length for most dolphin is 8 inches, but I've got a 10-incher for the big fish. Good knives such as Dexter Russell and a Forschner can be expensive but worth the price. The best knife I ever had was a $7 Forschner regrind I bought at a *Florida Sportsman* show.

Some people avoid meat around the stomach lining, bony areas and red meat down the centerline. By filleting fish a little different, you can get all the good meat without much waste. Cut from the shoulder as far down as the start of the rib cage. Carve completely around the stomach cavity being careful never to penetrate the internal organs, which can secrete digestive fluid onto a fillet. Then complete the cut down through the tail, whacking off the last 4 to 6 inches of stringy meat in the tail.

Placing fillet skin-side down, you should be able to see where the lateral line runs down the fillet. Starting your cut right on the lateral line, push the catch and re-ice it. The bottom of the box is lined with 3 inches of ice. Add a layer of fish. Add another 3 inches of ice, then another layer of fish. You get the picture.

Once we hit the dock, the bottom of a dock cart is lined with ice and the procedure begins again. Never let your fillets warm to outside temps, the meat will stay much firmer when you clean it.

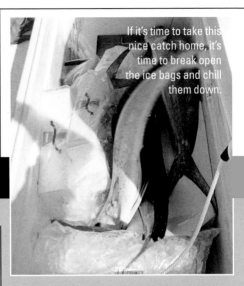

If it's time to take this nice catch home, it's time to break open the ice bags and chill them down.

dark meat along the center line.

knife down close to the skin and flare it out. You'll avoid 90 percent of everything that makes a fish taste strong. Do not run the knife all the way to the skin. Leave a fraction of meat on the skin to avoid blood or skin membrane in your meat. If you've been skinning dolphin by pulling the skin off before filleting, you'll be much happier with the quality of your fillet when you cut the membrane off and throw it away with the skin.

After rinsing fillets, that's the last time they should see fresh water. Fresh water (remember, it's good to wash our reels with) breaks down saltwater fish flesh. Freezing your fillets in fresh water means you'll be serving a soft, mushy fillet.

If your family eats a ton of seafood, a vacuum-packing machine is very handy. If you're going to freeze seafood more than a couple times a year, you really need to think about one of the new vacuum packers. If you're caught without one, you can improvise with a bucket of water and a quart-size freezer bag. Fill the bag one-third of the way with dolphin. Pack it down tight so there are no air pockets under the fish. Next, close the bag all the way across until there's just enough open-

ing to fit your finger in. If you force the bag down into water while holding your finger barely out of the water. You'll provide a vacuum seal as you pull your finger out and seal the last quarter inch of the opening just as the bag goes underwater. It's not perfect, but it will keep your fish from freezer burn for at least a month.

To Skin or Not to Skin

Peeling the skin off dolphin is a popular way to clean them. It does however leave a membrane just inside the skin on the meat. I think it's a much tastier fillet if you fillet the fish, then cut the skin off, leaving the membrane on the skin.

Dolphin can be cooked a lot of ways, and *Florida Sportsman's* own Vic Dunaway is legendary at cooking it. Let's look at a few of his favorites:

Spicy Sauté Amandine

- 2 pounds fillets
- 1 egg
- 1 cup milk
- Flour
- ½ cup butter
- ¼ cup almonds, sliced
- 2 tbsp. Worcestershire sauce
- Juice of 2 lemons
- Salt and pepper

Salt and pepper the fish.

Beat egg and milk together. Dip fish in egg-milk mixture and dredge in flour.

In skillet, melt butter and sauté fish at medium heat until brown on both sides.

Remove fish. Add almonds to skillet and brown. Add lemon juice and Worcestershire sauce. Pour over fish. Serves 3 or 4.

Blackened Dolphin

- Fish fillets
- 1½ tsp. cayenne pepper
- 1½ tsp. paprika
- 3 tsp. salt
- 1 tsp. onion powder
- 1 tsp. garlic powder
- ½ tsp. white pepper
- ½ tsp. black pepper
- ½ tsp. oregano
- ½ tsp. thyme

Mix all ingredients thoroughly. Coat single-serving pieces with olive oil or melted butter and then dip or dust them liberally with the blackening mix.

Classic blackened fish requires a cast iron skillet, which is allowed to get nearly red-hot. At that point, a half-stick of butter is dropped into the pan, followed an instant later by the fillets, which are cooked no more than two minutes a side. Add a bit more butter after turning, if needed. This approach, obviously, will create so much smoke that it's almost imperative to do the cooking outside.

An alternate method will allow you to stay in the kitchen—just barely—while turning out a blackened product that few would be able to tell from the "real" thing. For this, you can use any kind of skillet. Cast iron is still preferred, but an aluminum pan with a non-stick finish will do fine. Turn your stove's exhaust fan on high, and then place your skillet on a burner also set on high. Add a quarter of a stick of butter or margarine and when the butter turns dark brown—nearly black—put in two to four pieces of oiled and dusted fish. Cook about two minutes on each side, maintaining high heat. If more fish remains to be cooked, add more butter and again allow it to turn dark brown before proceeding.

Mushroom-Parmesan in the Microwave

- 1 pound fish fillets
- 4 ounces mushrooms
- ¼ cup onions
- 1 tbsp. butter
- ½ tsp. salt and pepper
- ½ cup sour cream, room temperature
- 3 tbsp. Parmesan cheese

Sauté onions until light brown.

Add mushrooms and sauté for two minutes more.

Arrange fish in a microwave dish with the thickest part in the middle. Spread mixture on top and microwave for 3 minutes on high.

Stir Parmesan cheese into sour cream and pour over fish. Sprinkle with bread crumbs and paprika.

Cook on high for about 3 minutes more. Let stand for 2 minutes. Serves 4.

Sautéed Fish with Vegetables

- 2 pounds fish fillets
- ½ stick butter or margarine
- Seasoned salt
- ¼ cup white wine
- 1 medium onion, sliced
- 3 vegetables (at least) from among the following:
- 1 stalk celery, chopped
- 1 small yellow squash, sliced
- 1 small zucchini, sliced
- 1 red or green pepper, sliced
- 1 ripe but firm tomato cut in small wedges

Sprinkle fillets with seasoned salt.

Melt butter or margarine in a large sauté pan at medium heat and continue heating until butter covers the bottom of the pan and turns dark brown.

Add fish fillets. Turn after about 30 seconds and brown other side for another half-minute. Remove fillets to a nearby platter.

Fish need not be done at this point, only browned on both sides.

Add onion and vegetables of your choice and cook, stirring frequently, until onion is opaque and other vegetables thoroughly heated. Do not overcook.

Sprinkle vegetables lightly with seasoned salt (or salt and black pepper). Add wine.

Place fish fillets atop vegetables, cover, reduce heat and simmer for about five minutes. Check fish for doneness.

All but the thickest fillets should be cooked. If not, simmer a few minutes more. Serves 4 or 5.

CHAPTER 20

Skunky. Scenarios

Why is it that it only happens on the days you get to fish? Why does it seem everybody else gets to go on the easy days? The days when the rips are plentiful and perfectly formed. Days when the ocean is calm and clear, and barracuda are nowhere to be found. Days when the fish are starving, and the living is easy.

The days you get to fish are quite a different story. On the days you get to fish, the water is either too hot or too cold. The wind is from the wrong direction, and the weeds that have been formed into perfect lines all week, are now scattered over hundreds of acres, just close enough together to make it impossible to troll through.

Forget the Saturday morning fishing shows full of fish catching euphoria, this chapter is about what we find far too often. We left the dock looking for utopia, but instead what we found is a skunky scenario.

Success is all about meeting the unexpected. It's about looking for deep blue, and finding slimy green. It's about having what you need, to overcome what you didn't expect.

Normally a throw back, this little guy following these whales might end up in the fry pan, if the day is tougher than expected.

Trouble Shooting

Having successful days fishing is often about the ability to overcome adversity. Make sure you're prepared when you run into conditions you didn't expect. Here are few common curveballs.

So much for your secret spot. Looks like the word is out.

PROBLEM: Too many boats. You ran 20 miles to get to the rip, but find it's rush hour out there.

ANSWER: Live bait. You're much more likely to catch fish with live bait on the weekend. A dolphin that passes up 100 trolled ballyhoo can't say no to a live sardine. I'd always prefer to fish an area by myself, but some days all the good spots are loaded with boats. If it's too far to go back inshore and catch sardines, the bar jacks and blue runners living under a pallet or weedline will bite a sabiki rig. Dolphin are suckers for these baits.

Time to boogie. When there's nothing to concentrate the fish, you're going to have to cover some water.

PROBLEM: You had your heart set on trolling ballyhoo or live bait along a rip that had been there for weeks. When you get out, there's no defined current rip to concentrate the bait and/or fish.

ANSWER: Never leave the dock without some small but heavy jets or concave-faced lures. If you don't have some feathers or skirted lures you can throw out at 10 knots-plus, you're going to find yourself trolling without covering enough water.

PROBLEM: Bonito. It's 10 a.m. on the rip, you're almost out of bait, and you're catching bonito four at a time.

ANSWER: Slow down, and strip out the bonito. Bonito (a.k.a. little tunny) like fast-moving baits and dolphin aren't as picky when it comes to trolling speed. Carry some salted bonito strips to back up your ballyhoo supply; put one out on a short. A fresh skipping bonito strip behind a ½-ounce Sea Witch offers a great hookup ratio. When an attacking dolphin bites down on a strip rig, it generally gets a mouth full of hook. You can also catch dolphin on soft-plastic shadtails or ballyhoo. Rubber squid and cedar plugs also belong in your box.

Turn the tables on bonito. When they chew up your ballyhoo, remember a fresh bonito strip makes an excellent trolled bait.

Never stop looking! These guys are looking for better water. They might want to put somebody in that tower.

ANSWER: Generally speaking, if you go farther offshore you'll find warmer water. You're often able to outmaneuver the cold water by heading east. The warm Gulf Stream water is out there somewhere. The colder the water inshore, the sharper the edge will be when you find the warm water.

PROBLEM: Coldwater upwellings. These generally occur when the waxing moon causes the Gulf Stream to swell, and the colder, deeper water pushed up against the continental shelf is forced upward, resulting in chilly surface temps in customary dolphin haunts.

Coldwater upwellings, no weedlines and full moons can al

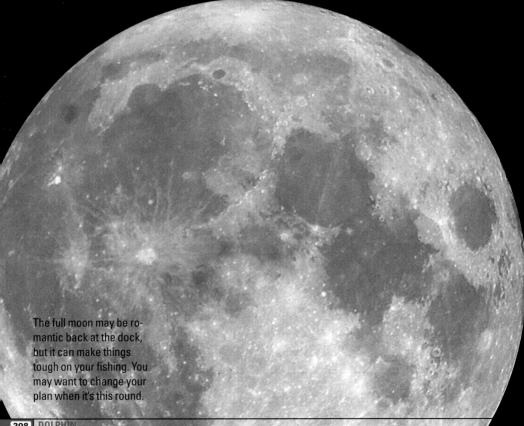

The full moon may be romantic back at the dock, but it can make things tough on your fishing. You may want to change your plan when it's this round.

PROBLEM: You run offshore and don't find any signs of birds, rips, weedlines or flotsam.

ANSWER: Don't forget dolphin are eating machines. If they can't find something to concentrate surface bait, they'll resort to hunting over bottom structure. Anything that will hold bait (wrecks, natural bottom) will hold dolphin and everything else. When the surface is barren, it's time to find temperature changes or bottom structure that are holding bait.

omplicate your day. Always have a Plan B.

PROBLEM: Full moon. It's hard to explain how full moons affect pelagic fish. The days just before a full moon are usually the best of the lunar cycle, but the day of the full moon and the few days after can be a real drag. The first few fish of a school might bite, but then the rest of the school shuts right down. A big fish might also run right up to your bait, but often will turn away. There seems little doubt that having enough light to feed at night keeps dolphin from feeding as aggressively in the daytime.

ANSWER: Hang around or leave a little later. They may start out the day full from partying the night before, but remember they're dolphin, and they won't stay full for long. Sometimes the action doesn't start until 4 p.m.

A recent "bailer" dolphin now calls for the gaff and a photo.

INDEX

DOLPHIN

INDEX

BOOKS Sportsman's Best: Book & DVD Series

The most complete series of how-to books and DVDs in print. Each book in the series has over 200-color photographs and easy-to-follow illustrations. Each book focuses on specific techniques, tackle options and tips from the experts and pros. Average book size is 240 pages. **$19.95 Ea.**

DVD (only)

The editors of Florida Sportsman and Shallow Water Angler fish with experts from Texas to Maine focusing on techniques that will help you, no matter where you live, catch more fish. Each DVD is professionally shot while fishing on the water. They're made to educate as well as entertain. Approx. length 65 minutes. **$14.95 Ea.**

* **Snapper & Grouper** * **Inshore Fishing** * **Sailfish** * **Offshore** * **Redfish** * **Trout** * **Dolphin**

Sport Fish Book Series *by Vic Dunaway*

* **Sport Fish of Florida** * **Sport Fish of the Gulf of Mexico**
* **Sport Fish of the Atlantic** * **Sport Fish of Fresh Water** * **Sport Fish of the Pacific**

Beautifully color-illustrated fish identification books. Food values, distinguishing features, average and record sizes, angling methods and more. **$16.95 Ea.**

Many FS/SWA Items also Available at Tackle and Book Stores.

DOLPHIN DVD

Sportsman's Best: Dolphin DVD brings the pages of this book to life. Join author Capt. Rick Ryals, the editors of Florida Sportsman magazine and some of the best offshore fishing captains in the country as they target the most popular ocean gamefish there is.

FEATURES

- ► **TROLLING 101**
- ► **USING FLOATS**
- ► **RUNNING AND GUNNING**
- ► **BALANCING YOUR TACKLE**
- ► **HOW TO RIG YOUR BOAT**
- ► **PITCH BAITS**
- ► **HOW TO RIG: SKIRTED BALLYHOO, SWIMMING BALLYHOO, BONITO STRIPS AND FEATHERS**
- ► **CLEANING AND COOKING**

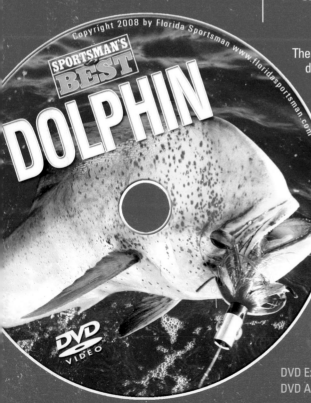

Copyright 2008 by Florida Sportsman www.floridasportsman.com

SPORTSMAN'S BEST DOLPHIN

DVD VIDEO

There simply isn't a better offshore gamefish; dolphin provide everything you could possibly ask for in a fish. They're constantly on the move searching for something to eat, they'll inhale just about anything thrown to or trolled by them, and they make spectacular, drag-screaming runs.

There's no better way to experience offshore fishing for this spectacular fish than being tied to one, but a close second is a well-produced DVD in High Definition. At least this way you get to pick your days when you're going to head out beyond the reef.

If catching a large dolphin is on your life list, this DVD and book are a must for you.

—*Blair Wickstrom, Publisher*

DVD Executive Producer: Paul Farnsworth
DVD Associate Producer: Matt Weinhaus